Better Homes and Gardens.

small space

decorating

WILEY

John Wiley & Sons, Inc.

Published by John Wiley & Sons, Inc., Hoboken, New Jersey
Published simultaneously in Canada

For general information about our other products and services, please contact our Customer Care Department within the United States at (800) 762-2974, outside the United States at (317) 572-3993 or fax (317) 572-4002.

Wiley also publishes its books in a variety of electronic formats. Some content that appears in print may not be available in electronic books. For more information about Wiley products, visit our web site at www.wiley.com.

ISBN 978-0-470-88710-3

Printed in the United States of America

10 9 8 7 6 5 4 3 2 1

Note to the Readers:
Due to differing conditions, tools, and individual skills, John Wiley & Sons, Inc., assumes no responsibility for any damages, injuries suffered, or losses incurred as a result of following the information published in this book. Before beginning any project, review the instructions carefully, and if any doubts or questions remain, consult local experts or authorities. Because codes and regulations vary greatly, you always should check with authorities to ensure that your project complies with all applicable local codes and regulations. Always read and observe all of the safety precautions provided by manufacturers of any tools, equipment, or supplies, and follow all accepted safety procedures.

contents

CHAPTER ONE

live

furniture

the living room is typically the first space people see when they enter your home, so it bears the decorating burden of making a good first impression. You want it to be inviting and comfortable for guests and reflective of your personality and tastes.

In a small living room, the temptation is to push all the furniture back against the walls in an effort to maximize floor space and make the room look bigger. But what you end up with is an uninviting, furniture-lined box.

It may seem counterintuitive, but pulling the furniture away from the walls—even just a few inches to make space for a floor lamp or sofa table— actually creates the illusion of greater depth and thus more space. Drawing seating pieces into the center of the room creates welcoming coziness that encourages conversation. Anchor the grouping to the room's natural focal point—a fireplace, a TV, a beautiful view. Or create a focal point by pairing the largest seating piece with eye-catching artwork that rivets attention.

If your small living room has a great view, outdoor access, or another natural focal point, orient seating so it doesn't get in the way of the main attraction, but resist the urge to relegate furniture to the perimeter. Here, the furniture is oriented toward the fireplace, and there is room behind the chairs for access to the French doors.

Seating is a priority in a small living room, but don't just aim for sheer capacity; offer intimacy, too. A fireplace makes a natural focal point for a furniture grouping. The love seats are armless, and the sofa's arms are slender, creating a less weighty look and freeing up visual space.

GLOSSARY:
SMALL-SPACE FURNITURE

Love seat: A short sofa made for two—hence the name. Pullout models accommodate overnight guests.

Armoire: A tall cabinet originally used as a wardrobe; it can also hide a bar or games and books.

Sofa table: Also called a console table, it's narrow and slightly lower than the sofa back. It's a good spot for a reading lamp.

Parsons chair: A slim, armless, upholstered piece that can adapt to different rooms and styles.

End or side table: About chair-arm height, it stands beside seating to hold a lamp, beverage, and other necessities.

↑ **It's OK to put furniture pieces close together.** This grouping maximizes intimacy, comfort, and convenience. Low-profile arms make the chairs easy to slip in and out of and create a less crowded look.

A clear acrylic coffee table practically disappears, creating the illusion of more floor space in front of the sofa. Acrylic's low visual impact and functional versatility make it perfect for small living rooms.

DESIGN BASICS:
SIZING UP A COFFEE TABLE

Don't go too small with a coffee table. A right-sized table spans about two-thirds the length of the sofa it serves. That's long enough to adequately anchor a furniture grouping while leaving room for traffic flow around both ends. Any accessories should fill out the tabletop without looking crowded, leaving room for beverages and other everyday objects.

In lieu of a low coffee table, a higher tea table offers more open space underneath, which is valuable real estate in a small room. Here, it's a spot for a bench that provides a footrest or extra seating.

storage

because the living room is usually one of the larger spaces in a small home, it has to carry a pretty big share of the storage load. And that means you'll want to use much of its wall and floor space for built-ins and freestanding storage pieces.

It's not that you need to cram the living room with your stuff. It's a matter of incorporating storage into the furnishings and decor. After all, the living room is where you spend a lot of time, so it makes sense that this is the room where you keep many of the things you use for entertainment and relaxation every day. It's the place for the TV and the remote, for books, magazines, and newspapers, and maybe CDs, DVDs, and DVRs.

The living room is also where you surround yourself with favorite objects—the less practical things you love and want other people to see. With a stylish mix of high-profile storage spots and hidden caches, your living room can be both livable and lovable.

MANAGE CLUTTER

It doesn't take much for a living room to look a little too lived-in. Try these clutter-control tips.

Clean up bookshelves: Overstuffed shelves create visual chaos. Edit items so you can alternate low stacks of books with groups of upright volumes. Showcase just a few objects between tidy rows of books.

Collect baskets: Humble baskets hide clutter stylishly. Store everything from your remote controls to linens in one, and place it under a coffee table.

Recycle magazines: A few look inviting. A few years' worth says "pack rat." Display the newest and nicest issues on a coffee table or in an eye-catching rack. Box or recycle the rest.

◄ **Try a fresh take on the coffee table** by placing storage cubes in front of the sofa. These dark wicker versions hold everyday items while anchoring the bold color scheme.

◄ **Let "double duty" be your mantra** when arranging a small living room. In this seating area, the bookcase provides storage while creating a partial wall and a back for the sofa, an armless model that enhances openness by maintaining a low profile. Drawers under the sofa cushions add closed storage to the mix.

► **For a more cottage or country look,** let a trunk, vintage suitcase, or cedar chest play the role of coffee table. This wicker trunk adds bountiful storage and rustic texture.

Armoires aren't just for bedrooms. In the living room, an armoire can be an entertainment center, an extra closet, or a library. The doors and drawers let you hide the contents when they're not in use, and the piece's finish can reinforce the room's color scheme. Here, its size also helps balance the weight of the fireplace. The coffee table is no storage slouch, either, with its cubbies holding slideout baskets.

Make storage an art form by choosing furniture pieces that are as striking as the objects they hold. The low stand beneath the TV provides open storage while matching the room's clean contemporary lines and bold black hues. One way to camouflage a flat-panel TV is to incorporate it into a wall of silhouette artwork. Hang the TV first, then arrange vintage picture frames painted black around it.

HOW TO:
HANDLE THE TV

Some consider today's sleek TVs to be works of art worthy of continuous display, while others would rather discreetly tuck the screen away when it's not in use. From a decorating standpoint, housing the TV in some type of armoire, cabinet, or media center gives you more options. If you like having the TV out in the open, consider a flexible seating plan that doesn't make the screen a full-time focal point.

Bookcases can hold more than books.
If your library is meager, have no fear—the built-in shelves represent a storage bonanza for keepsakes and collectibles. A doored cabinet below hides less show-worthy items.

If you've got books, flaunt them.
Built-in bookshelves (or a set of freestanding store-bought units) create an intimate library corner in a small living room. Keep the look orderly by aligning the book spines with the edge of the shelves—and no stacking books and papers on top of the neat rows!

Decorative trays provide pretty, portable storage where you need it most.

windows & light

a key to making your small living room feel warm and inviting is keeping it bright. Small spaces tend to be dark ones, too, and when a lack of square footage meets a lack of light, cozy can turn claustrophobic. However, when natural light and artificial illumination work together, a small room can feel much bigger.

Take a quick lighting inventory of your living room. Note which direction the room faces and where the windows are. You can't easily change those factors, but you can change window treatments and arrange furniture to take better advantage of the light you have. At night, count the fixtures, note their locations, and assess the mood of the room. Too dark? Too cold? Can you read easily? Are the walls and furnishings shown in a flattering light? Many living rooms rely on a single overhead fixture, but layers of light—ambient, task, and accent—make a living space look and feel its best.

Natural light and stylish fixtures work together to make a modest living room feel more spacious. Draperies and walls reflect the light. Lamps are positioned for reading.

Add height and drama to windows by hanging curtains high and wide around the openings—start about 3 inches below the ceiling or crown molding. Add to the illusion of a taller window by hanging a blind right under the curtain rod.

DESIGN BASICS:
TREATING WINDOWS

The way you dress windows in a small room—if you dress them at all—can affect its perceived size. Generally, the simpler the window treatment, the better.

Bare windows create a clean look that shows off the architecture and opens up the space. At night, however, they can become black holes. Blinds or Roman shades offer an unfussy solution, providing privacy day or night and light control during the day.

Simple drapery panels soften the architecture of the room without crowding the space. To make windows seem taller, hang draperies just below the ceiling; to widen windows visually, extend draperies beyond the window frame. Fabrics that match walls enlarge the room.

If your view is less than ideal, frost the panes or apply window film so only space-enhancing light comes in. Floor lamps are a good fit for a small room—no extra tables needed.

walls & ceilings

you may face expanses of painted drywall or plaster in your living area. Although you could leave the surfaces that way—and you may have to, depending on where you live—consider your options. A new paint color energizes tired walls. Wallpaper is another option, offering patterns and textures not possible with paint. Either way, you can boost the wow factor of a diminutive room by covering just one wall.

Install beaded board for a vintage or country look. For a more formal effect, add chair-rail molding about 32 inches above the floor and create faux panels in the upper section with molding or strips of lath. Such treatments add depth and architectural distinction without cluttering.

If you have standard-height ceilings, you may want to paint them a light color and leave them alone. Crown molding and a ceiling medallion around a light fixture can dress up a dowdy ceiling, but keep them in scale with the room. Save fancy treatments such as a faux-coffered effect for high ceilings.

HOW TO:
RAISE THE CEILING

Keep it clean: Paint the ceiling a light color and, if possible, avoid mounting a fan or ceiling light.

Extend the wall color: Painting the ceiling to match the walls can create the illusion of a higher ceiling. Paint crown molding to match, as well.

Right-size furniture: The ceiling seems farther away when you're sitting in low chairs. Yet, tall armoires and bookcases urge the eye upward, and that creates the illusion of height, too.

↑ **Give walls architectural character** with wainscoting. The paneling can extend as high up as you want. Here, it's extra-high to accommodate a deep ledge for art.

← **Use patterns to add pizzazz to walls,** such as the one in this modest-size living room. The tone-on-tone wallpaper creates energy without overpowering the room.

→ **A vaulted ceiling adds vertical volume,** making a small room feel larger. Keeping the ceiling color light enhances the effect. Vertical stripes on the wall stretch the room, too. Crown molding picks up the wood tone of the floor.

color

Conventional wisdom dictates that dark colors make a petite room feel smaller, while light colors enlarge it. Dark colors demand attention and warm colors advance toward you, thus bringing the walls closer. Soft neutrals are quieter and recede. Color is about emotional impact, however, and sometimes mood trumps size.

If you like drama or intimacy in your living room, paint the walls a deep color and accent it with crisp white trim. (The legendary interior decorator Billy Baldwin famously painted his tiny Manhattan apartment entirely in high-gloss chocolate brown.) If you prefer an airier feel, try soft yellows, greens, or grays. Even white need not be sterile—it comes in many shades, and you can create a serene mood by using different whites for walls, ceiling, and trim.

Of course, color doesn't just apply to walls. Upholstery fabrics, window treatments, furniture, and accessories all import mood-setting, space-enhancing color into a small room and imbue it with personality.

Full-bodied colors create a 3-D effect. In this room, the red in the chair, the gold in the sofa, and the green in the wall art stand out from the chocolate brown walls and drapes. Shades of those three colors repeat in other elements, so they don't seem random. The contrast between the white woodwork and the darker wall color adds more depth.

It doesn't take a big splash of color to give a living room personality. If you want to leave the walls white—or if you have to—find ways to incorporate a more vibrant color into furniture and accessories. The red of the glass display cabinet and small table in this space energizes without overwhelming, providing color with openness.

It's OK to have fun with color. In a small space, sassy hues in stripes and plaids spice up traditional looks. Give the eye a place to rest by incorporating swaths of quieter color.

Instead of using white walls as a backdrop for colorful furnishings, try the reverse approach shown here. The green wall color connects the room to the scenery and spaciousness outside.

DESIGN BASICS:
PICKING A WALL COLOR

To make a space-smart wall-color change, let a favorite fabric be your guide, even if you're starting from scratch. Choose the furnishings for the room first, then use one fabric to cue your wall color. Any fabric suggests at least three options for wall colors—a matching shade, a lighter shade, and a darker shade. Each will produce a different feeling in the room, yet all will complement the furnishings.

Mixing patterns and colors creates depth and adds interest to a living room.

Limited space need not limit your color palette. The gold walls here provide a warm, sunny backdrop for vivid accents of cerulean blue and leaf green, with shades of lighter, grayer blues and greens for variety and depth. Repetition keeps the accent colors from seeming spotty, but it's the expanse of yellow walls and draperies that anchors the room and pulls the disparate hues together.

art & photos

for personalizing blank walls, it's hard to beat displaying favorite art and photographs. But there's more to it than pounding a nail in the wall and hanging the picture level. Pleasing wall arrangements rely on the same interior design concepts involved in placing furniture. And they're even more important in a small room, where wall space is limited.

Pay attention to rhythm, balance, and weight. Rhythm is the movement from one object to the next. Balance is the even distribution of visual weight within a display. An unbalanced arrangement may look top-heavy or bottom-heavy, which can shrink a room. An object's visual weight—its perceived mass—might demand that it be displayed alone. Anything that is large, dark, bright, boldly patterned, or oddly shaped needs some breathing room.

Sometimes, negative space—the wall area between items—is as interesting as the items themselves. Like white space on a printed page, negative space creates a clean look and keeps the room feeling spacious.

If you don't want to put holes in your walls, you can still display photographs attractively. Lean them against the wall on a shelf, or use stand-up frames. The overlapping treatment on this fireplace mantel creates depth.

Functional objects can be art, too, as with these mirrors displayed in a grid. They give the impression of a larger space by reflecting light and outdoor views. Though the mirrors look vintage, they are actually new pieces of glass distressed with acid to look old.

HOW TO:
HANG ARTWORK

Gather the pieces you want to hang. Cut out matching shapes from paper and tape the shapes to your wall to determine the best arrangement. When you're ready, drive the picture hook or nail through the paper, then tear it away to hang the artwork. Try hanging pictures low enough to link them visually to furnishings or aligning them with an architectural element, such as a window or door.

Favorite artwork can set your living room's decorating style. The bold graphic wall letter echoes in the geometric shapes on the sofa pillows, while the small tables are like little sculpture pieces.

fabrics & pillows

k nowing a little about fabric goes a long way toward making your small home live large. All kinds of fabric elements—upholstered furniture, rugs, pillows, throws, window treatments, even wall-coverings—make a small space more comfortable and colorful.

When choosing fabric, especially for upholstery, keep in mind that neutral colors and patterns will stay in style longer than trendy hues and prints. Neutrals also take the backseat and let your accessories shine. If you do want bold pattern in your upholstered pieces, use it on the smaller items. Rugs, pillows, and throws are easier to switch out, so go bold with those.

When ordering upholstered furniture, get a fabric swatch first and live with it for several days and in different kinds of light. Try to get your hands on a picture of the piece upholstered in your chosen fabric, too. A stripe or floral that looks good on a swatch may overpower a small living room when it covers an entire sofa.

Charcoal sofa fabric and a well-sized rug add texture while making a chic neutral backdrop for vibrant pillows. The pillow colors repeat in accessories for a cohesive look.

DESIGN BASICS:
RULES FOR RUGS

Use a rug to inspire the look and color of the entire room.

Be brave. Pick a rug with personality and let it be artwork on the floor.

Measure carefully before making your final rug choice.

Don't undersize. Too much exposed floor shrinks a room.

Combine rugs. Can't find a large rug you like? Pair two smaller ones for a big look.

Use a pad to protect floors, hold the rug, and cushion feet.

Place furniture within the rug's border or just touching the edge.

Nervous about big fabric patterns?
Putting a large-scale pattern on the floor lessens its impact, since a rug isn't at eye level and is partially concealed by furniture.

DESIGN BASICS:
FABRIC TRENDS

Cotton: Tightly woven into canvas or sailcloth, this natural fiber resists wear, fading, and pilling.

Mohair: This luxurious natural-fiber fabric is durable and wrinkle-resistant.

Velvet: Made from natural or synthetic fibers, it has a short, dense pile that is luxuriously soft to the touch.

Faux suede: Made of polyester, faux suede is much more affordable and easier to clean than real suede.

Linen: It tends to wrinkle and is not that durable or easy to clean, but it looks natural and is eco-friendly.

Hemp: A plant-derived fiber, hemp is washable, durable, and just as eco-friendly as linen.

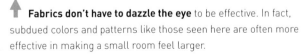
Fabrics don't have to dazzle the eye to be effective. In fact, subdued colors and patterns like those seen here are often more effective in making a small room feel larger.

White walls and upholstery balance the impact of color and pattern in this space.

Strip away the fabrics from this room, and it's mostly white space. Rugs, pillows, and valances power a lively take on traditional style. In small doses, busy fabrics energize a petite space without overpowering.

big things—the sofa, chairs, the coffee table, and the TV—make the living room functional, but it's the little things that make it personable. Be careful not to have too many "little things," however, to avoid a cluttered look.

Just about anything can be an accessory, from simple vases of flowers to elaborate vignettes of your treasures and trinkets. There's no science to accessorizing, but it is an art with some techniques.

For example, if you spread accessories throughout the room, keep the walls simple and quiet to focus attention on the objects. Likewise, if you want the eye to focus on the shapes and textures of accessories, keep their colors neutral or monochromatic.

Coffee tables and end tables are natural spots for accessories. Remember, there's style strength in numbers. Small objects standing alone can look forlorn, yet in a grouping they sing.

◀ **A handful of well-chosen accessories** is all it takes to give a small living room the sophisticated style of a larger space. Take advantage of natural display spots, such as the coffee table, end tables, and the fireplace. Here, the hearth is perfect for a classical bust.

▶ **Bookcases are a great place for accessories,** as treasures make character-filled complements to the volumes on the shelves. Lean large items, such as plates and framed artwork, against the backs of the shelves. Books stored horizontally become platforms for objects.

▼ **A traditional fireplace mantel begs for accessories.** And in a small room, a mantel provides an opportunity to go vertical, which stretches the space visually. In this case, blooming branches and framed vertical photographs accentuate height.

HOW TO:
DRESS UP A FIREPLACE

The easiest way to accessorize a fireplace mantel is to center one large item on or above the mantel and flank it with a series of smaller items on either side, creating symmetry. To avoid boring stiffness and unify the pieces, overlap the smaller items so that one or two approach the front edge of the mantel and one or two move toward the back.

CASE STUDY #1
personal style

A no-rules approach to decorating guided the owner of this charming Craftsman-style bungalow as she made it her own. Armed with a set of tools, an eye for bargains, and a knack for mixing styles, the homeowner preserved the vintage bones while refreshing the rooms with color and a blend of traditional and contemporary elements.

1 **An oval table in the dining room** offers the friendliness of a round shape and the seating capacity of a rectangular one. Divided-light windows convey the home's Craftsman character, as do an original light fixture and cabinets with 1930s lines. The red accent color on the ceiling links to a chair in the adjoining office.

2 **A blend of slick, nubby, and shaggy textures** keeps the living room's neutral palette interesting. Orange accents repeat throughout the space, from the wall art and pillows to the flowers and the coffee table's wood tone. The art is designed to stimulate conversation.

3 **Vintage-look elements** give the small bath big doses of charm and character. The outside of the old-fashioned tub was painted black to complement new tile in a Craftsman-style pattern. The wraparound shower curtain rod is a period touch, as is the high-rise showerhead fitting. An antique table warms up the utilitarian space with a furnished feel.

4 **Beaded board is hard to beat** when it comes to creating a vintage vibe. If your small bath's walls aren't blessed with that surface, prefinished wainscoting panels are an economical option and easy to install. Original crown molding in this home inspired the architectural mirror and shelf. The rounded pedestal sink is a space-efficient choice.

5

5 Small kitchens can have islands, too. The compact version here provides a wealth of storage, as well as prep space on top and places to hang linens. If even a small island crowds your kitchen, get one that's on wheels and roll it away when not needed. Painting the cabinetry a brilliant shade of white creates a look that will never go out of style.

CHAPTER TWO

cook

cabinets

t he biggest part of any kitchen, in both function and style, is the cabinetry. It's where you store the things you need to prepare meals and what covers most of the walls. The cabinetry is what people notice when they walk in. In a small kitchen, cabinetry takes on even more importance. It has to provide a lot of storage in a little space, and it typically occupies a higher percentage of the square footage than in a larger kitchen.

If the cabinets you have are in good shape, you may want only to freshen them up with paint, try a different door treatment, or replace the hardware. If your cabinets are beyond repairing or refreshing, consider replacing them.

In choosing cabinetry, focus on door styles and finishes. Do you prefer a plain slab front, a recessed panel, or a raised panel? Clean lines or ornate detailing? The finish can be natural wood, stained or painted wood, or a glaze over stain or paint. Inside, look for adjustable shelves for flexible storage, pullout trays, and full-extension drawer glides that increase storage space.

Changing one or more of your cabinet doors can open your space by breaking the solid expanse of wood. Try one of these ideas:

Be clear. Outfit a solid door with a clear-glass panel for an open look.

Frost it. Instead of a clear-glass panel, install a frosted version that hides clutter better.

Get wired. Replace a wood door panel with wire-mesh grillwork for an old-world look. Chicken wire says country-style.

Hang fabric. On a base cabinet, take off the doors and hang a curtain across the opening. You'll add color, pattern, and a soft touch.

Picture it. Personalize cabinet doors by using them to display photos. Frame snapshots in mats cut to fit door panels.

Chalk it up. With chalkboard paint, turn a cabinet door into a mini blackboard for messages.

Go doorless. Remove the door entirely for instant openness.

⬅ Cabinets don't have to be in boxy rows. Varying the height and width of upper cabinets increases storage flexibility. Here, the extra-tall units stretch the space vertically, while frosted-glass doors lighten the look.

⬇ If you want a contemporary-look kitchen, choose slab-style cabinet doors that fully cover the frames and pair them with long, slender pulls. A dark finish adds drama and picks up the brown tiles in the backsplash for an impression of continuous color.

➡ If you want a classic-look kitchen, it's hard to beat crisp white cabinets with simple recessed-panel doors and drawers. Here, the upper cabinets extend all the way to the ceiling, providing extra storage space.

You can put things on top of cabinets as well as inside them. Open space atop these upper cabinets is ideal for displaying a colorful assortment of plates, vases, and pottery. Utilizing high-up space is an easy way to liven up basic brown cabinets without changing them.

Open storage keeps a small kitchen from feeling confining. Shelves take the place of upper cabinets in this space, while a cabinet with textured-glass doors provides bonus storage without totally blocking the window. Removing the doors from two base cabinets and replacing them with fabric curtains brings pattern and softness.

HOW TO:
PAINT KITCHEN CABINETS

Clean cabinets with detergent to remove surface oils, then sand lightly to scuff the wood. Priming before painting is critical. Use a good water-base primer. After priming, apply two coats of paint. Use a latex paint formulated for cabinets. It's OK to brush it on, but for the smoothest finish, use a sprayer. This means removing the cabinet doors and taking them outside or to the garage.

Open shelving in place of upper cabinets makes a small kitchen feel more open.

A mix of open and closed cabinetry lets you decide what to show and what to hide. Bookcase-style shelving creates the illusion of a roomier kitchen because your eye has farther to travel before it reaches the wall.

appliances

just as a kitchen isn't a kitchen without cabinetry, it's not one without appliances, either. Hardworking appliances supply the power needed to cook, cool, and clean. But they can also power the decorating scheme, especially in a small kitchen, by showing off their sleek metallic finishes or hiding behind cabinetry-matching panels.

Fortunately, whichever look you prefer, you can find appliances to fit smaller kitchens. Refrigerators and ranges come in 24-inch-wide models, and dishwashers—normally 24 inches wide—are available in 18-inch-wide versions. Drawer-style dishwashers help in small kitchens as well.

A big decision is whether to buy a range—a combined cooktop and oven—or keep the cooktop and oven separate. The main refrigerator decision is where you want the freezer—on the top, bottom, or side.

When choosing a dishwasher, consider the noisiness of the unit. In a small home, a quiet dishwasher is a little luxury that makes a big difference.

Small ranges can do big-time cooking. The 24-inch-wide model shown here was designed to serve serious cooks living in an apartment or a loft with limited kitchen space. Though the range doesn't take up much room, it features a gas oven, four full-size burners, and professional-grade styling.

Getting the microwave off the counter and into a built-in niche frees up precious prep and serving space in a small kitchen. Here, an undercounter spot lets the appliance anchor a breakfast station.

Coordinate appliances and cabinetry to minimize or maximize the visual impact of appliances. Here, the refrigerator's color is close enough to the cabinetry finish to keep the appliance from standing out. Stacked wall ovens save space in a small kitchen.

HOW TO:
HIDE APPLIANCES

Appliances are workhorses, but not everyone thinks they're showhorses. If you'd rather downplay the machines in your kitchen, try these strategies.

Cover appliance fronts with cabinetry-matching panels.

Buy counter-depth appliances that fit flush with cabinetry.

Install refrigerator drawers or dishwasher drawers under the counter in lieu of full-size units.

Tuck the microwave in an appliance garage or wall niche.

Choose a smooth cooktop with burners that aren't obvious.

Use downdraft ventilation to eliminate the need for a hood.

countertops

there's no shortage of options for kitchen countertops—they're available in a variety of materials. But choosing the right countertops is tricky because they pull double duty: They must survive the daily abuse of kitchen prep work while making a style statement. And in a small kitchen, where counter space is limited, that statement has to be concise.

There are few quick fixes for existing counters you don't like. You either learn to live with them or replace them. Marble and granite are premium upgrades. However, a little of these luxury surfaces goes a long way in a small kitchen, so they can be a smart splurge.

Solid-surfacing, quartz-surfacing, and other stone look-alikes are generally more affordable, easier to care for, and come in a broader palette of colors than natural stone. Laminate and ceramic tile are the safest and most economical options for a small kitchen, while stainless steel, concrete, and glass tempt you to push the style envelope.

DESIGN BASICS:
COUNTERTOP PROS & CONS

Laminate: Though thin, it's economical and offers almost limitless options in colors and patterns.

Wood: A great choice for vintage-look kitchens. The color range is limited by nature. High-maintenance.

Stainless steel: Provides a contemporary look and a neutral color that suits today's appliance finishes. Expensive to install but rugged.

Natural stone: Granite is the gold standard in counters, marble a classic choice. Either way, it's a splurge, but not so much in a small space.

Solid-surfacing: Like stone in thickness and look but easier care and more color options. A bit pricey.

⬆ **Wood counters are a popular choice** because both the surface and the look stand the test of time. To let the wood develop a natural patina, avoid cleaning it with abrasive chemicals. Instead, wash the counter with warm, soapy water and rub it with mineral oil once a month.

⬅ **The subtle gray hues in this marble countertop** complement the white cabinetry and beaded-board walls, while still maintaining an open and clean feeling throughout the space. In a small kitchen without a lot of countertop space, marble is often worth the extra cost. Many bakers like to have just one slab of it for rolling out dough.

➡ **Stainless-steel countertops not only blend well** in most color schemes, but they're also bacteria-resistant, making them a favorite of health-conscious homeowners and restaurant chefs alike. The reflective industrial sheen is something of a space expander.

storage

just finding places to store everything is a challenge in a small kitchen. Cooking calls for lots of ingredients and gear, and it's easy to accumulate new items faster than you get rid of old ones. If you're suffering from a storage shortage, start by paring down, if possible. Get rid of what you don't really need or use. If you can't toss it, at least get it out of the kitchen.

Then start looking for ready-made storage remedies. For example, a host of inserts and add-ons—pullouts, roll-outs, tray dividers, and adjustable shelves—can give existing cabinets a storage boost. Or purchase a compact rolling island that tucks out of the way when you're not using it.

Search throughout your kitchen for slivers of stealth storage. Space at the top of your sink's base cabinet—those few cubic inches right below the counter—can be mined for tilt-out storage. Near the floor, the toe-kick is often just tall enough for shallow drawers. And never underestimate the power of a well-placed shelf.

For storage with maximum openness, consider restaurant-style shelves like these. They let you see at a glance where everything is stored, and the commercial look is a striking alternative to cabinetry.

Look both high and low for storage solutions. This kitchen has its share of upper cabinets, but it also offers storage closer to the floor, including the bottom of the island cart and open shelves below the end of the peninsula. The shelves are rounded to echo the countertop.

Open storage turns everyday items into decorative elements while adding visual breathing room. Glass-front cabinets and baskets in open shelves let color, pattern, and texture pop out.

HOW TO:

FIND A KITCHEN DESIGNER

The smaller the kitchen, the more creative you have to be in finding storage solutions, and professional designers have that creativity. Designers have experience with spaces similar to yours and access to products that you can't buy in stores. They know that you want storage solutions that are attractive as well as functional.

To find a kitchen designer in your area, start by visiting the web site of the National Kitchen & Bath Association, *nkba.org*, which certifies kitchen and bath designers. You can search for designers by zip code and within a certain number of miles.

You may also find professional kitchen design help at a local home center or showroom.

 In a kitchen too small for an island, a rolling cart can play the same role as needed. In this space, the stainless-steel cart matches the finish of the appliances, making the temporary helper fit right in.

Pot racks work well in small kitchens. There are many design variations, but the idea is to keep pots and pans within reach when you need them and away when you don't.

backsplashes

t he backsplash—that space between the countertop and upper cabinets—is primarily functional, protecting the wall from spatters and splashes. But over the years, the space has evolved into a style showcase. In many kitchens, the backsplash is like a theater marquee, an eye-catching billboard that grabs your attention and brings you in.

In a small kitchen, the backsplash presents perhaps your best opportunity to do something personal and fun. The safe approach is to extend the countertop material up the wall several inches, and there's nothing wrong with that. However, you're missing an opportunity to inject color, pattern, sheen, and visual rhythm in a high-profile spot. All of those elements can help your kitchen look bigger—and more interesting.

Though ceramic tile is the traditional backsplash surface, natural stone, beaded board, and stainless steel are all good alternatives. Glass-mosaic tile—similar to ceramic but more shimmery—is especially popular today.

Tile is a time-tested backsplash surface, but you're not limited to rows of single-color squares. Here, trim pieces in three colors are arranged in a lively version of an eye-catching basket-weave pattern.

Stainless steel works well on a range or cooktop backsplash. The contemporary-look surface matches today's professional-style appliances and is easy to clean.

Tile backsplash incorporates the color of the wood cabinetry, creating a pleasing sense of visual harmony.

Go as high as you like with the backsplash. To be functional, it may only need to rise several inches, but you can extend the surface all the way to the ceiling to maximize the visual impact.

Subway tile is classic. The traditional look is 3x6-inch white ceramic tiles in a running bond pattern. Here, glass tiles in a gray-green hue convey a more modern feel. Their translucence and reflectivity open the space.

Tile isn't the only practical backsplash surface. Painted beaded board works well, too. Its vertical lines flatter a small space and instantly convey cottage charm. Here the light blue color provides a pleasing contrast to the white shelves and nicely complements the dishware on display.

HOW TO:
SET A FOCAL POINT

A focal point is a spot in a room to which the eye is naturally drawn. It's what people see first. You can create a focal point by including an element that attracts attention through one or more of these qualities: size, color, lighting, and "wow" factor. In a small kitchen, an excellent focal point is the backsplash, especially the area surrounding a range, cooktop, or hood, where there tends to be more wall surface.

sinks & faucets

n a small kitchen, you still have lots of options for faucets and sinks that are both functional and stylish. The National Kitchen & Bath Association recommends a 22x24-inch single-bowl sink for a small kitchen, but if you generally hand-wash dishes, a 22x30-inch double bowl is more convenient because it gives you one side for washing and the other for rinsing. The standard 8-inch-deep twin basins don't accommodate large cookware well, but you can find models with one larger basin for dishwashing and a smaller one for food prep. The size of your base cabinet will also help determine how large a sink your kitchen can handle.

With faucets, size isn't much of an issue. As long as the faucet is the right size and configuration for the sink, you're free to focus on style and finish. Take advantage of that to choose a faucet with a really distinctive appearance—think oil-rubbed bronze finishes, high-arc spouts, restaurant-style sprayers, sleek single-handle designs, or vintage-style curves.

A farmhouse sink with a bridge-style faucet is the perfect pairing for a vintage-look kitchen. The curvy spout and lever handles are also appropriate period touches.

Single-handle faucets work well in contemporary kitchens. The sleek, minimalist design of this model echoes the sculptural look of the long cabinet pulls. The sink itself suits the geometry of the kitchen, a space full of prominent squares and rectangles.

For a commercial-look space, consider a faucet with an institutional-style sprayer. The exposed stainless-steel sink, stainless-steel countertop, and open storage add to the chef-ready ambience.

GLOSSARY:
KITCHEN SINK MATERIALS

Stainless steel: Newer, thicker models are quieter than their less expensive predecessors. Finishes range from a mirrorlike shine to a satin luster.

Cast iron: Enamel fired on an iron form is heavy-duty but may chip, exposing the iron to rust. It's very heavy to install.

Composite: Made of crushed granite or quartz mixed with resin, these sinks resist stains and scratches and take the heat better than solid-surfacing. The color selection is limited, and they can be expensive.

Vitreous china: More common in baths, this glazed clay is hard, nonporous, and stain-resistant but can be damaged by dropped objects and abrasive cleaners. Fireclay, also a glazed ceramic, is more resistant to heat and scratches. It mimics cast iron but won't rust if chipped.

Solid-surfacing: It's a hardwearing acrylic material that is easy to clean. Scratches and burns are easy to remove with gentle sanding. It can be damaged by hot pans and can be expensive.

lighting

kitchens in small homes can be fickle. Sometimes they call for lots of light, and other times not so much. If you're chopping vegetables, you definitely want to see what you're doing, but if you're having a cozy dinner for two, you want more of a warm glow than a harsh glare. That's why it's important to provide light from multiple sources, such as recessed ceiling cans, pendants, wall sconces, undercabinet fixtures, windows, and skylights. By being able to control how much light is applied where, you make your kitchen feel as intimate or spacious as you desire. Dimmers are a good way to gain that control.

But there's a decorative side to kitchen lighting, too. A fixture in a high-visibility spot—such as above a sink, table, or island—helps set the style for the space, so give careful thought to what it looks like. The best lights boost a room's style quotient even when they're off.

DESIGN BASICS:
PENDANT POWER

Pendants—light fixtures suspended from the ceiling by rods or cables—put light where needed without overpowering a small kitchen. Increase their versatility by putting them on pulleys. That way, you can raise and lower the fixtures for different tasks and accommodate people of different heights. As a general rule, the bottom of a pendant should hang 30 inches above a table or countertop.

A pendant with a short rod allows close-to-the-ceiling mounting that draws the eye up and provides good overall lighting. In a small kitchen with abundant natural light, a single ceiling fixture may suffice.

Some kitchens call for bold lighting, such as these bronze-finish pendants that convey an industrial look while pooling light where it's needed most: over the island cooktop and eating counter.

Installing an eye-catching fixture as a centerpiece over an island or table does as much for the room's personality as it does for the lighting. Here, a Moravian star makes a big decorating impact in a small kitchen.

flooring

flooring—though not as dazzling as appliances and cabinetry—is one of the most important choices in a kitchen. You'll spend much of your kitchen time standing, so the surface needs to be comfortable underfoot. The floor will be exposed to heavy traffic, messy spills, and falling objects, so it also has to be durable. In a small home, flooring helps differentiate spaces that aren't separated by walls. And the shapes and sizes of the individual pieces can stretch the kitchen visually.

Lifestyle, design tastes, and your budget will help narrow your flooring options. If stone and hardwood aren't in your budget, there are plenty of alternatives that still provide remarkably impressive results. For example, ceramic and porcelain tile do an amazing job of mimicking natural stone, while engineered wood and laminates come prefinished, are less subject to temperature and humidity changes than real wood, and typically cost less. They're also easier to install, especially for DIYers.

Though expensive, wood floors have much to offer. They look warm and traditional, and the direction of the grain helps shape the lines of the room.

No matter what kind of floor you have, mats and rugs in high-traffic areas will reduce wear by catching a lot of the dirt and other abrasive debris that gets tracked in. Plus, rugs can add patterns and textures.

DESIGN BASICS:
KITCHEN FLOORS

Here's a quick look at some of today's top flooring options for your kitchen.

Ceramic tile: Water-resistant; comes in many colors and patterns. Can be slippery.

Hardwood: Rich, warm, and natural, but pricey. Long, narrow boards serve to lengthen rooms.

Laminate: The look of wood in a durable, affordable form. Can't be refinished. DIY friendly.

Stone: Naturally beautiful and durable, but often hard, cold, and expensive.

Vinyl: Cushy, economical, and easy to clean. May discolor, scratch, and tear. DIY friendly.

A cheerful checkerboard floor energizes this kitchen with its lively pattern and high-contrast colors.

A dark floor adds needed visual weight to a mostly white kitchen.

personal touches

taste matters in a small kitchen—and not just when you're cooking. The way you decorate the space is an opportunity to make it reflect your personal tastes, a chance to incorporate tile, wallpaper, art, and other elements in a way that makes the kitchen more than a utilitarian room.

Start with the sink. Switch out a plain white model for something more decorative, like a hand-painted basin with a vibrant tile surround. The range backsplash is another perfect space to add whimsical artistry. Select art that fits the color scheme of your kitchen, and hang it proudly to be admired every time you cook. You can even have photos reproduced onto ceramic, glass, or tumbled-marble tiles and use them on the backsplash.

Dressing up plain cabinet doors with decorative hardware is another easy way to add a personal touch. Knobs come in designs such as fruits, vegetables, and animals, and in many mediums, such as glass, pewter, brass, and nickel.

This kitchen gets a color infusion from the eye-catching orange cabinetry and the earthy browns of the wood backsplash. It's a combination that energetically conveys the homeowner's unique personality.

A crystal chandelier shares air space with a small pot rack for a touch of unexpected glamour. More creative touches: a divided backsplash that's a mirror below to expand the sense of space and a blackboard above for notes and shopping lists.

Dancing between classical and modern, this kitchen dares to be distinctive by conveying both elegance and informality. It successfully blends traditional elements—such as the island light fixture and marble countertops—with the playful shapes of contemporary stools.

DESIGN BASICS:
WHITE KITCHEN

White is a natural choice for small kitchens—it's bright, fresh, and clean, and light bounces off the glossy tiles, countertops, and painted cabinets to expand the sense of space.

Use shades of white to avoid utilitarian sterility and create a sense of depth. Choose a dark flooring, such as espresso-brown wood or wood-look laminate, to ground and warm your kitchen.

Bring in bright or bold colors with accessories or with tile accents on the backsplash. Any kind of hardware will work with white, so you can choose a finish that helps convey your decorative style, whether cottage, traditional, or modern.

compact charm

This 200-year-old bungalow was a real fixer-upper, but a couple used their design talents and carpentry skills to make it their first home. The quirky little cottage is full of small-space smarts and personality.

1

2

3

1 **Tall, narrow upper cabinets raise the small kitchen's ceiling** while mimicking old-fashioned freestanding cupboards. Simple café curtains stitched from pillowcases add color without subtracting light.

2 **The compact living room boasts 12-foot-high ceilings,** so artwork is stacked to suit the strong vertical orientation. The coffee table is a library cast-off that had its legs sawed down to size.

3 **A round dining table is small-space friendly,** as its shape makes it easier to gather and maneuver around in tight quarters. Vertical stripes on the chrome dining chairs are good space-stretchers, too.

4 **Vertical wood strips make the bedroom look taller.** The molding pieces and the fresh blue color add cottage character and charm as they mask imperfections in old walls of plaster and plywood.

5 **A drop-leaf table in the short hallway** to the bath turns a sliver of space into a focal point. The warm wood tones repeat in the bath, where a French footstool keeps towels handy

6 **In a small home that lacks a defined entry,** just a bit of space by the door is enough for a storage and display area that will be appreciated by people coming in and going out.

7 **The tiny office is carved out of converted porch space.** A pretty fabric skirt hides a printer and file boxes stored below the desktop, while shelves take full advantage of the high ceiling.

CHAPTER THREE

eat

tables & chairs

because a dedicated dining room is often a luxury in a small home, it helps to be flexible about where you eat. Whether your space is a formal dining room, informal dining room, or kitchen, the table you choose needs to be large enough to allow adequate elbow room for diners and a height that's within comfortable reach of the chairs. The standard height for a dining table is 29–30 inches.

Not all tables are dining friendly. Check leg placement for proper support—a leg at or near each corner, a center pedestal, multiple pedestals, or trestles. Dining chairs should have fairly upright backs so that diners can sit comfortably close to the table and still have back support. The upright look stretches the height of a small kitchen, too.

Chair arms should be low enough that the chairs slide under the tabletop. Leave adequate space between the apron (the skirtlike extension under some tables) and your thighs.

← **Transparent "ghost" chairs,** made of polycarbonate, provide style and function while remaining practically invisible. The clear chairs open up the room, as does the mostly white decor.

▼ **Dining chairs don't have to match.** Dark wood shades unite the chairs, and lively fabric colors and patterns freshen traditional shapes.

GLOSSARY:
DINING CHAIR STYLES

Chippendale: Based on 18th-century British design, a style noted for elaborate splats (center back supports). May have ball-and-claw feet.

Ladder-back: Also called Shaker. Plain-style chairs with horizontal slats on the backs. Seats may be woven from rush or tape.

Parsons: A fully upholstered chair with a fairly tall, straight back and linear design. The seat may have a skirt that falls to the floor.

Queen Anne: Recognizable by the shaped crest rail (top of back) and urn-shape center splat.

Regency/Empire: Inspired by Greek forms, this 19th-century style includes chairs with scrolled arms and backs, as well as Duncan Phyfe's delicate klysmos chairs with curved backs, horizontal or lyre-shape splats, and reeded or saber legs.

Windsor: An early English style characterized by legs and spindles driven into the seat. Variations include bow-back and hoop-back.

↑ **A table with distinctive character** makes meals special. This one has a stone top and slender iron legs, conveying an old European feel. The long, narrow table doesn't crowd a modest-size room.

Benches maximize seating capacity in a small dining area and convey a casual picnic-table feeling.

◄— The next best thing to alfresco dining is a spot with views. Furniture, fabrics, and tabletop items bring in the browns and greens of nature. Windsor chairs grace the ends of the table, while cushions soften the benches.

—► Going unarmed can be liberating. Armless chairs and a cushioned bench squeeze a lot of seating into a little space. Fabrics help the chairs blend into the walls, making the corner look more open.

◄— Turn the table for a better fit. This dining area shares space with the living room, so smooth traffic flow was important. Positioning the long, narrow table to echo the rectangular shape of the room lets people pass by smoothly. An area rug helps define dining boundaries.

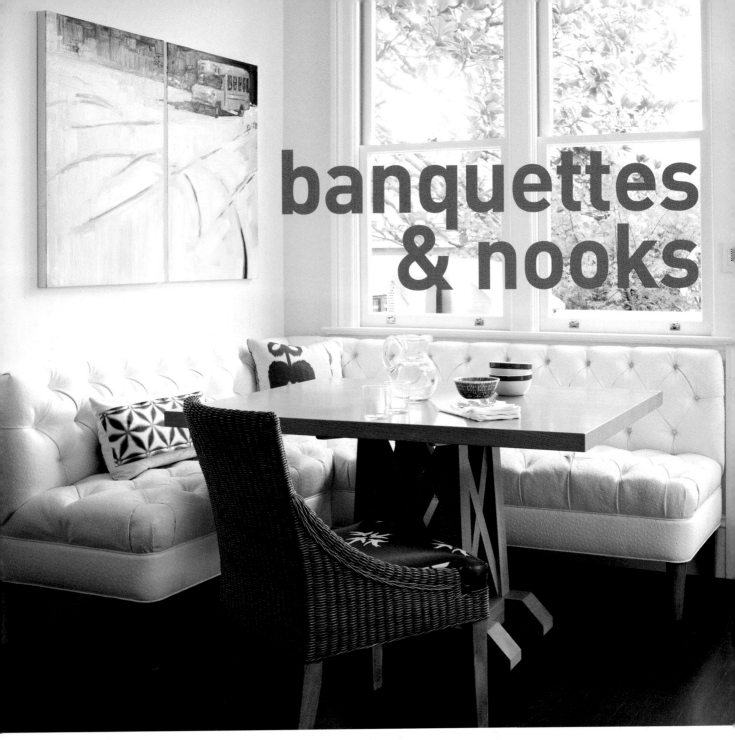

banquettes & nooks

breakfast nooks provide inviting spots for meals and conversation while saving on space. And they're not just for breakfast. You can host friends for lunch or dinner, or even stage a family game night. A banquette—a built-in bench—lends a restaurant-style feel to your dining nook while providing great storage opportunities under the seat. Depending on the configuration of your space, you can design the storage as cabinets, drawers, or a chest that's accessed by raising the seat. If your banquette is more formal and sofalike, turn the space below into storage with neat baskets.

Limited space need not limit creativity. Dining nooks can be adapted to fit any decorating style. Make the space your own by boldly showcasing curios or a favorite painting, or try covering your banquette with a fabric that complements the wall color—this creates a visual flow that makes a small space feel less confining.

Anchoring your nook near a large window helps give the impression of space and light. The wood tones of the wicker chair and wooden table contrast with the upholstered bench fabric. The painting and hand-sewn throw pillows offer splashes of vibrant color.

Window seat plus table equals a quick-and-easy breakfast nook. Bring in some painted wicker chairs for a lighthearted garden or seaside cottage style.

DESIGN BASICS:
SIZING UP AN EATING NOOK

Before deciding on the table and seating for your nook, make sure the setup provides enough space to comfortably sit, eat, and maneuver in and out. Ideally, diners should have 18–24 inches of space between them, with at least 3 feet of clearance between the table and wall for chairs to slide in and out and for people to walk behind. Banquettes eliminate the need for that extra clearance space.

Breakfast nook tables and seating can be hip, not square. This one features a mod-look round table and the curves of classic Eames chairs for a retro contemporary vibe. A fun clamshell light fixture and colorful fabrics and accessories add to the lighthearted spirit.

Custom-built benches can hide spacious storage wells under the seats—just allow enough clearance between the seat and the table to allow access. This table's single metal pedestal leaves plenty of leg room for adults and kids and keeps the space looking open.

kitchen dining

having a small kitchen can seem limiting if you want it to include space for dining, but it doesn't have to be. While you may not be able to serve large meals in your kitchen, creating a comfortable eating space that serves two—or maybe a few—is very achievable.

Armless chairs, stools, or benches alongside a narrow table or counter space allow for adaptable and fun dining within arm's reach of the kitchen. Eat-in spaces broaden a small kitchen's function—rather than being exclusively focused on food prep, it becomes a hub for people.

Accessibility and portability are the most important components of functional dining space in tight quarters. Don't try to fit a too-large table and chairs into a cramped kitchen. It will just make the space seem smaller. If you plan to move your table often, non-marking swivel casters on your table will ease the task. The same goes for lightweight stools—it's no problem to relocate them temporarily.

A small wood-topped island does double duty as an extra prep surface and an eating spot for two. Armless stools maximize space efficiency.

A table on casters or rollers lends mobility to your kitchen eating space. See-through chrome bar chairs take up little space visually and are easy to move where needed.

HOW TO:
SIZE DINING STOOLS

To ensure you select right-height barstools for your table or countertop, measure the height of both the prospective stools and the eating surface, which could be at standard table height (30 inches), counter height (36 inches), or bar height (40–42 inches). For comfort, leave a 10–12-inch space between the top of the barstool and the dining surface, as well as a 3-inch space on either side of each stool.

In a tight kitchen, a narrow table is an ideal addition. It works as a useful staging area, an extension of countertop space, and an intimate spot for meals.

lighting

romantic low lighting is common in restaurants. The old joke is that it's done intentionally so you can't see the food—or the menu prices. But dining by candlelight (or its electric equivalent) also encourages diners to relax and conversation to flow, and if you're having friends over for dinner, you want to set a convivial mood. Whether you illuminate the dining table with a sparkly chandelier or a row of contemporary pendants, be sure to install a dimmer switch so you can control the light level.

If you use your dining room table for breakfast and lunch as well as dinner, you'll want to take advantage of daylight for natural illumination. Abundant daylight helps convey a sense of spaciousness and brightens the mood indoors. To maximize the light your dining area receives, consider dressing the windows with shades or blinds mounted above the window. This allows you to pull the shades all the way up during the day but lower them at night when the windows become black holes.

HOW TO:
SIZE A CHANDELIER

Measure your table to determine the right-size chandelier for your room. If you have a rectangular or oval table, subtract 24 inches from the length and 12 inches from the width to find the diameter of the fixture. For a round or square table, choose a fixture that's one-half to three-quarters the table's width.

Regardless of ceiling height, hang the fixture 30–32 inches above the tabletop to spread light so you're neither blinded by glare nor lost in shadows.

◀ **Bold color is less risky in a small room** when the space is bright. Light from unadorned windows keeps the wall of red—a color said to stimulate the appetite—from devouring the room.

◀ **Natural light bathes this dining room,** with the white walls, ceiling, and armless chairs all helping to expand the perceived dimensions. The traditional-look chandelier is sized well for the long table.

➡ **A 1960s-style chandelier** partners with a sleek modern table and classic 1950s Eames chairs to enliven a traditional kitchen-dining area with a funky sense of style. Color bridges the gap between design eras.

Great natural light and a focal point fixture let a kitchen shine by day or night.

storage

getting tableware within easy reach of the dining area can be a challenge in a small home. Even if you have a dedicated dining space, it likely offers little wall space for storage or floor space for freestanding furniture pieces. However, there are strategies you can try to create more dining storage.

One approach is to utilize corners. Corner hutches eat up little floor space, yet a pair can stow almost as much as a full-size breakfront. For a built-in look, buy unfinished versions and finish to match the trim in the dining area. You can also make use of vertical space. Stackable storage modules offer even more flexibility than stock kitchen cabinets.

Or look to an adjacent room. If your dining room adjoins the kitchen, trade the shared wall for a two-layer storage system: 24-inch-deep units on the kitchen side, 12-inch-deep units on the dining side. Carve out a pass-through in the center so the kitchen counter can double as a sideboard.

← A weathered china cabinet lets any kind of dinnerware take on the character of family heirlooms. The distressed finish complements the bench at the table.

↓ A hutchlike built-in stands nearly flush with the wall, its recessed shelves providing traditional-look storage without squeezing clearance space around the table.

DESIGN BASICS:

DINING STORAGE

If you have room for storage pieces in your dining area, here are some types to consider.

Sideboards, servers, and buffets: A combination of cupboards and drawers with a table-height surface for food. Long sideboards on tall, slender legs evoke 18th-century styles. More compact pieces with one or two drawers above a two-door cabinet reflect 19th- and 20th-century designs.

China cabinets: A tall glass-enclosed top section of shelves for displaying china with drawers below for linens.

Hutches and corner cupboards: A fusion of display space and closed storage. Shelves are usually open rather than protected by glass doors. Hutches and corner cupboards let you show off dinnerware, glassware, and serving pieces, freeing space in the kitchen.

Specially designed dining room furniture isn't a necessity, however. A set of bookshelves, a dresser, or a console table can be pressed into service as storage and serving space, and a curio cabinet can put your china on display.

↑ **Decorating with multitasking in mind** lets this dining room double as a library or office. Floor-to-ceiling bookcases, wicker chairs, and treasured collectibles allow flexible function.

◀ **Built-in storage in the dining area** saves space. Lower shelves put everyday items in reach, while higher levels hold special-occasion glassware. Blinds and chair backs mimic the lines of the shelves.

▶ **A table with built-in storage** is a great choice for a small dining area. The drawer and shelf under this one can hold condiments, linens, or utensils. The contrast between the natural wood table and distressed white Napoleon chairs creates an eclectic look.

decor

table space and seating are all it takes to have a functional dining area, but you need more than that to make the space inviting and stylish. Color, fabric, and accessories personalize the space and enhance the dining experience for you, your family, and guests.

Let's say there's a fabric in a window treatment or chair cushion that complements dishware you collect. The coral color you pull from that fabric could become the new wall hue and inspire your flower selections for tabletop centerpieces. Or in a room with soft green walls, you could keep that color and decorate the table with botanical motifs and greenery. On the windows, simple white cotton panels would maintain a light, fresh feel.

Glass is a great decorating choice throughout a small dining area. It's transparent and airy, letting light pass through and helping a room feel more spacious. The table itself can be glass, and you can top it with wineglasses, candle hurricanes, and water carafes.

⬆ **Favorite objects are virtually fail-proof** when it comes to cueing a decorating scheme. In this dining room, the lamp and the vintage sign suggested a sophsticated black, white, and red color combination. The table's natural wood finish helps moderate the high color contrasts, and the top is decorated in simple fashion to keep the red from overpowering.

⬅ **Topiaries are great table toppers,** conveying a natural look in a highly decorative way. They suit the rustic style of this dining area, which takes advantage of a dark wall color to let a white bench and chairs pop out.

➡ **Multiple elements may inspire decor.** Here, the walls draw a color from the painting, but the reddish-brown in the sofa and pillows echoes the wood tones of the floor. This is an example of creating a custom dining area on the fly—a traditional sofa plays the part of a banquette, with a pedestal table and chairs pulled up to it.

Stylish upholstered chairs can give any casual dining area a sophisticated look.

CASE STUDY #3
sizing it up

Urban living presents decorating challenges—and opportunities.
For example, this townhome's 1,600 square feet were spread out
over four floors. But space-saving moves and smart use of color,
light, and furnishings help the home succeed on all levels.

1

2

1 **Built-ins create attractive storage and display areas** in the master bedroom. A fireplace with a stainless-steel surround replaced an awkward closet that had made the room feel smaller.

2 **Bamboo trellis-pattern wallpaper** stretches the perceived dimensions of the living room and plays off the bamboo flooring. Wall mirrors work like windows to open the space.

3 **The dining area makes a high-style statement** while offering space-saving features. Banquettes seat 10 people and include storage drawers underneath. There's even space for a dog bed. The mirror is a decorative focal point that enhances the impact of the lights.

4 **A bright green wall color with white trim** calls attention to under-the-stairs storage. Custom-built shelves under the stairs glide out to provide access to items at the back. Replacing the panel in the nearby closet door with a mirror reflects part of the kitchen and doubles the apparent space.

5 **Painting exposed ceiling beams white** is a way to keep an interesting architectural feature from weighing down the room. This kitchen is probably big enough for a small island, but going without one makes the space feel more open and easy to navigate. The peninsula assumes the island's role of multipurpose prep and serving spot, doubling as the back of the banquette to save space.

CHAPTER FOUR

bathe

sinks &
vanities

a functional sink that suits your needs makes your morning and evening routines hassle-free. But a beautiful sink makes those routines enjoyable. In a small bath, choosing a sink style means weighing priorities. A pedestal sink, which rests on a slender floor stand, is space-efficient but offers little storage. Small wall-hung sinks take up less space but have the same storage problem. Console sinks, which rest on legs or stands, offer the same openness with the benefit of shelving.

If you like your sink surrounded by a counter, go with a self-rimming (drop-in) model. Undermount sinks, which avoid a dirt-trapping rim, put more visual emphasis on your counter. Vessel sinks, basins that sit atop the counter, are the most striking but may cause more splashes on the counter.

If you prefer cabinetry under your sink, make sure handsome doors and drawers open to hardworking storage space. An attractive option is to turn a piece of furniture—such as a dresser—into a vanity.

DESIGN BASICS:
BATH MIRRORS

Behind every great bathroom sink and vanity—or somewhere close, at least—you should find a stylish mirror. Mirrors are especially important in small baths. Besides playing their basic role of grooming aid, mirrors amplify light and space in tight quarters.

Instead of settling for a plain rectangle or mirrored medicine cabinet, consider designs that will personalize your bath. Oval and round shapes, mosaic tile frames, beveled edges, and etched glass are all options. Flank one with a pair of pretty sconces. And if you don't have room for an over-the-sink mirror, find one that extends from the wall on a swing or accordion arm.

Striking surface choices make a sink and countertop stand out big-time in a small bath. The pairing of a sleek stainless-steel basin with a rough-hewn wood countertop—seemingly just cut from the tree—is a memorable mixing of manufactured and organic.

Console sinks are a good small-space solution, offering a design that is compact and open but with opportunities for storage. Here, a stainless-steel shelf under the sink holds linens without looking as closed-off as cabinetry.

Out-of-the-ordinary sink and faucet designs create a natural focal point in a small bath. This one features an infinity sink, a vessel-style look in which a raised slab directs water to the basin's perimeter channel. If that's not eye-catching enough, the wall-mount faucet penetrates a mirror.

A stool can be squeezed into a tight bath for seating and a pop of color.

If a white wall-mount sink seems too institutional, soften it with a fabric skirt. It can hide less attractive items stored below and lets you add a little color and texture. These sinks offer little or no storage space around the basin, so use wall-mount holders for essentials.

Vessel sinks turn a basic bath function into an art form. The above-counter basins can take many shapes and be sculpted from a variety of materials, such as the natural stone shown here. Though the look is a splurge, a vessel sink does save space—it can hug the backsplash, as it's typically paired with a wall-mount faucet.

Exposed plumbing adds to the vintage charm of a console sink, especially when polished chrome legs match the finish of the pipes. Though the sink, toilet, and shower are close together, the mostly white decor keeps this small bath from looking crowded. Black accents provide a sharp contrast to the sea of subway tile.

tubs & showers

t he right tub or shower can transform your small bath from a crowded utilitarian space to a comfortable, stylish room in which to relax. And if you can't replace the fixtures you have, you can probably enhance them by freshening the bath's decorating scheme.

With space at a premium, a basic question is whether or not you need both a tub and a shower. If you rarely soak in the tub, consider removing a bulky built-in tub/shower combo in favor of a shower-only enclosure. This can open up significant wall space, leaving the room feeling larger. A clear glass shower door adds to the sense of increased space.

Or if you prefer a tub but are stuck with a blah or off-color built-in model, a new surround can brighten and freshen the look. Replacing the tile or other wall covering around the tub is much easier and more affordable than replacing the tub itself.

A handsome deck and elegant surround boost the appeal of a basic built-in tub. With the shower in its own space, the tub needs no curtain or door, so the look is open.

A freestanding tub can make a small bath feel more open by creating separation from the walls. In this bath, a high-arc faucet that comes up through the floor pushes the vertical dimension, adding to the sense of spaciousness. Freestanding tubs call for storage nearby, and that's a chance to do something stylish, such as a pretty stool.

A small shower can be fun and fashionable, too. The cylindrical version in this bath tucks into a tight corner while catching the eye with its circular base, halo-like rod, and ceiling-mount rain showerhead. A deep vessel sink mounted on a small wooden table packs a lot of function and style into a compact space.

HOW TO:
SIZE YOUR SHOWER

Adding a shower enclosure may not take up as much bath space as you think. Most building codes require a shower to be at least 30x30-inches, although the National Kitchen & Bath Association recommends at least 36x36 inches. Allow at least 30 inches of clearance space in front of the shower for access. Using a curtain or bifold door on the shower instead of a hinged one saves space, too.

storage

you can never have too much bath storage. Towels and washcloths need to be close, and toiletries, grooming supplies, and medications need to be stashed somewhere—and preferably in an organized way so you see what you have and know when to restock.

One strategy is to think vertically. Tall storage pieces offer more volume in tight spaces than shorter ones, so think multi-level. Perhaps a wheeled, multi-drawer cart near the vanity is what you need. Or maybe a tall, narrow shelving unit on the wall makes more sense. You could fill the shelves with oversize baskets to maximize storage and style.

Sometimes you just have to steal space wherever you can. That might mean using a corner bookshelf and filling it with bowls of bath supplies and stacks of rolled bath towels for an attractive and functional display. Or build nooks right into the wall between studs. An unused area above the toilet fitted with simple glass shelves can offer ample space for toiletries.

Though pedestal sinks are great space savers in a small bath, they don't offer much storage. This design solves that problem stylishly by pairing the sink with a built-in bank of drawers.

A small bath with two sinks calls for shareable storage. The handsome center cabinetry in this vanity area is easily accessible from either side, plus the tall, narrow unit makes good use of vertical space.

The space beneath a console-style sink can be mined for storage. Here, the console design offers a countertop and drawers around the sink, with flexible space below. In this case, baskets store linens where they're needed and yet preserve much of the open look.

Even the smallest bath has a door, and as long as it swings open (instead of folding or sliding), it offers storage space you can tap without making permanent changes. Attach adhesive-backed lightweight metal hooks to the back of the door to hold towels. Or install removable over-the-door racks and bins to store extra towels and shampoo.

⬆ **Paneling runs horizontally** across the cabinet doors in this snug bath, subtly creating the illusion of greater width. The all-white environment, anchored by a dark countertop and floor, makes the most of the abundant natural light to enlarge the sense of space. And who cares about a small bathroom anyway when you have such a spectacular view?

⬆ **A double vanity can work in even a modest space** when you consolidate storage on a single wall. In addition to the abundant base cabinetry, a counter-level hutch echoes the look of the backsplash as it supplies both open and closed storage at a convenient height.

Vertical thinking turns a sliver of wall space into a storage gold mine.

⬆ **A pair of pedestal sinks can anchor a stylish small bath for two.**
The sinks hug the wall and don't crowd the room with boxy vanity
cabinetry. Medicine cabinets offer space-saving storage, as does the
ladderlike shelf unit.

lighting

lighting illuminates the darkest corners of a small bath while creating a calming ambience. Without adequate light, your bath can appear much smaller and feel less comfortable than it should, and you may have a hard time with tasks such as shaving or applying makeup.

To brighten your small bath, try finding a vanity mirror with lighting already built in—or frame your existing mirror with sconces. Mounting sconces directly on mirrors can create a dazzling show of reflections that will increase the room's perceived size. Focusing low-wattage indirect lighting on the ceiling can create the illusion of a higher ceiling, too.

Visually merge indoor and outdoor spaces by taking advantage of abundant natural light from windows and minimizing window treatments. In a bath with boxy cabinetry, let light fixtures supply delicate curves and fancy flourishes. But if your bath features an ornate furniture piece, keep the lighting sleek and subtle to avoid diverting attention away from it.

Positioning the vanity beneath a window provides plenty of space-boosting natural light by day. Shapely contemporary sconces become the primary light source when night falls, their wall-hugging shapes blending into the subway tile.

Abundant daylight brightens this compact two-person vanity arrangement by way of a skylight. When the sun isn't shining, two sconces and an overhead fixture provide illumination. Sconces high on a wall—five to six feet from the floor—will project the light and may reduce the need for additional lighting.

A pair of traditional-style sconces frame the vanity mirror in this narrow bath, providing a soft glow that complements the light from the window. Although generally used for indirect and accent lighting, sconces serve a task-lighting role in the bath, brightening the vanity to help with grooming.

HOW TO:
CREATE STYLE WITH SCONCES

Sconces take up little room, but they make a big decorative impact. Use them to accent a mirror, brighten a vanity, or warm a bare wall. The easy-on-the-eyes light is welcome in a room full of cold, hard surfaces. Many have shapely shades that create a pleasing halo on the wall. In a small bath, a single sconce in a dark corner chases away shadows and leaves the room feeling warmer.

tile

durable and resistant to water, tile has traditionally been the surface of choice for bathrooms. What's more, tile comes in many shapes, sizes, and colors, offering a variety of ways to create interest, especially in a small space. Though tiles can be made of natural stone and glass, ceramic tiles are the most popular choice for baths because they're so adaptable and affordable.

Tile can color as much of the bathscape as you're comfortable with. It can totally cover the walls and floor, or you can save it for the wettest zones, typically the sink backsplash and the tub or shower enclosure.

Tile can also be as plain or as fancy as you'd like, from basic white squares to embossed, hand-painted, or glass designs. Mosaic tiles are a favorite in small baths, as their petite patterns don't overwhelm a modest swath of wall or floor space.

A mix of tile shapes and sizes enhances the style of this small bath and suits its scale. Mosaic tile maximizes pattern on the floor, while black trim pieces set off subway tile on the walls.

Mosaic tile is beloved in baths, as its small-scale patterns seem to stretch the dimensions of walls. In this space, the tile cues the color scheme, and the mosaic look echoes in the vanity front and the mirror frame. White grout complements the countertop and toilet.

Don't get carried away with colors and patterns. In a small bath, both will really resonate. With less distance between walls, there's more "bounce." Here, confining the vibrant tile to one wall harnesses its energy wisely, with white surfaces calming the rest of the room.

DESIGN BASICS:
SMALL-SPACE TILE TIPS

Bath tile comes in a range of sizes, from tiny 1x1-inch mosaics to pieces as large as 24x24 inches. Though larger tiles have become popular on bath floors, take care when considering them for a small space. With large tiles, there's little room for pattern repeat and the size of the squares can overwhelm the bath visually. If you do choose tiles larger than 12x12 inches, stick to a solid color or a subtle pattern. Small tiles work well, but that does mean more grout lines, and all those lines call for more precise installation and more vigilant cleaning.

A big advantage of having a small bath is that your tile budget stretches further. There's little exposed floor space, so it doesn't take many tiles to cover it. A material or design you thought too expensive may be worth the splurge when you figure how few tiles you need. Similarly, if you tile most of a wall or backsplash with inexpensive field tiles, just a few fancier tiles sprinkled here and there will have a huge impact on the room—and require only a modest boost to your budget.

fabrics

fabrics in the bath soften and warm hard, cold surfaces. In a small space, layers of fabrics add needed depth, and some fabric patterns can help stretch the room's dimensions. All fabrics provide a degree of color and texture, plus they're easily changeable when you want a new look.

Shower curtains are a prime example. In most small baths, the shower curtain is the largest expanse of fabric, so it carries a lot of visual weight. You can stick to something clean and simple to set a calm tone, or you can make the curtain a focal point by choosing a bold color or pattern. A lively shower curtain pattern can often compensate for a blah tub and surround.

Don't forget window treatments. Even if your bath has only one small window, a fabric treatment can make it look taller and wider. And lightweight fabrics provide privacy without blocking the natural light that keeps small spaces feeling open.

If you have a standard tub/shower combo, a shower curtain is less visually confining than sliding doors. Here its large pattern also balances the tiny mosaic tiles.

Fabric is a quick small-bath refresher when you can't change the fixtures or walls. Here, a fabric shower curtain picks up colors in the wall paint and accent tile.

This curtain is more like a room divider, setting off the tub area as a separate room within the bath. The white fabric creates a sense of solitude for the bather but doesn't block out the natural light from the window.

The fabric shower curtain cues the hues of accessories.

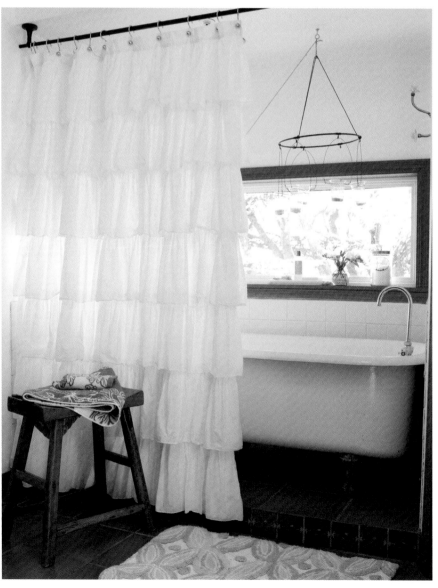

DESIGN BASICS:
BATH LINENS

Beyond choosing the style of your bath linens, you also have to choose the material. For everyday towels, look for 100 percent cotton. High-end towels are made of long-staple Egyptian or Turkish cotton or pima. Grams per square meter (GSM) indicates the fabric's density. A higher number means a thicker towel.

Going green? Look for organic cotton, hemp, and bamboo. Bamboo has anti-bacterial qualities, and both bamboo and hemp are mildew-resistant.

A natural cotton alternative is the European-style waffle-weave towel. The smooth finish is fuzz-free and absorbent, and the towel dries quickly and gets softer with each washing.

sinks & faucets

faucets hold a steady job in a small bath, working hard during the morning rush and again before bedtime. If you have only one bath in your small home, that faucet will be noticed, so you want it to be fashionable and functional. There are numerous styles but just three basic design configurations.

Single-handle (or single-lever) faucets allow for simple water-temperature control and easy cleanup—there's only one spot to collect grime. And when inches count, a compact single-handle faucet leaves more space around the sink.

Two-handle faucets offer variations such as cross-shape and lever handles. Widespread models measure 8 inches from handle to handle, but mini-widespread faucets are only 4 inches across, making them a good choice for small baths. For maximum space savings, wall-mount faucets accommodate shallow vanities and work well with vessel sinks.

GLOSSARY:
FAUCET FINISHES

Black: Maximum drama. Good against vibrant patterns and with wrought-iron accessories.

Bronze: Conveys a rustic or old-world look. Oil-rubbed is the best known of its variations.

Brushed chrome: An update on tradition that mutes chrome's sheen for a more modern look.

Brushed nickel: Matte finish for a soft sheen. Goes well with white and stone surfaces.

Hammered nickel: Like brushed nickel but rougher and hand-wrought. Craftsman-esque.

Polished brass: Best known in the glamorous gold, mirrored form that has been in and out of style.

Polished chrome: A classic that goes with just about any look. Conveys vintage charm well.

Polished nickel: Similar to polished chrome, but has more of a soft amber tone. Can tarnish.

⬆ **A single-handle faucet creates a sleek, contemporary look.** Paired with this compact wall-mount sink, the single-handle faucet frees up precious inches around the rim of the basin. The faucet's shiny finish matches the gleam of the sink's attached storage rack.

⬅ **Wall-mount faucets are real space savers.** They're also good for conveying a clean, modern look, especially with the minimalist spouts and handles shown here. The minimalist-style faucets add to the spacious feeling of this modest-size double vanity.

➡ **Bridge faucets are a vintage design,** but they work with more contemporary vessel sinks, too. Bridge faucets feature separate hot and cold valves that rise well above the countertop and are connected by visible plumbing. The combo is twice as nice in this bath, where the double vanity is compact but doesn't feel crowded.

furniture & accessories

ncorporating freestanding furniture pieces into your small bath adds character and personality, making it feel more like a decorated room and less like a collection of fixtures. Freestanding pieces can also make a small space feel less confining than built-ins sometimes do.

You don't need to buy new furniture for the bath—flea market finds work, or you can repurpose pieces you already have around the house. For example, a dresser or chest of drawers that looks boring in a bedroom can easily become a focal point in a small bath. With a little carpentry work and a fresh finish, either piece could make a stunning vanity.

Furniture adds storage as well as style. Hutchlike pieces with glass-front doors, open shelves, and drawers can hold a lot of items and display them attractively. Where you can't alter walls, furniture pieces may be the only way to boost storage. And they need not be big. An old milking stool takes up little room, yet it imparts character and serves as a seat.

Repurposed pieces bring function and style to a bath. The open shelves of a dining room hutch keep necessities in easy reach, a rustic wooden ladder turns into a wall-hugging towel rack, and a fabulous architectural mirror creates a stunning, space-expanding focal point.

Glass-front cabinets open up small spaces. This piece looks like something salvaged from a doctor's office or hospital pharmacy, but a fresh hue and sleek hardware give it new life for bath storage use.

A tall table from an entry hall or foyer supplies a slice of sophisticated storage in this cozy bath. The table's height and long legs play up the room's vertical dimension, as does the wallpaper. The table is also open underneath, echoing the design of the console vanity.

Arranging assorted flea market finds like these in your small bath creates a casual cottage feel with a rustic, eclectic edge. But the pieces aren't just for show—they each serve a function.

CASE STUDY #4
simply stylish

Carved out of former church space, this 1,100-square-foot condo is a comfortable sanctuary full of natural light, calming colors, and built-in storage. Simplicity is the big theme that makes the small space work.

1 **An exterior view of the 1873 building** reveals distinctive architectural character, including a steeple. The condo shares the site with a bank, restaurant, and shoe store.

2 **A pair of adaptable chaise lounges** provide space-saving seating in the main living area. Shelves under the stairs roll out to reveal a hidden closet, while the coat closet to the right conceals a relocated water heater.

3 A curved and carved Victorian headboard adds architectural character to the bedroom, where calm colors prevail. A rolling unit serves as a storage piece and a room divider.

4 Removing a small vestibule opened up the entry and living room, creating space for built-in bookcases. The wall quote is from James Joyce's *Portrait of the Artist as a Young Man.*

5 Having the shower and sink share a wall saves space in the bath. The glass shower doors and console sink design foster a feeling of openness, as does natural light from above.

6 The old steeple deck of the church, on the condo's upper level, is now a cozy getaway space bathed in natural light. The extra-long chaise is comfortable for reading, thinking, or napping.

3

4

5

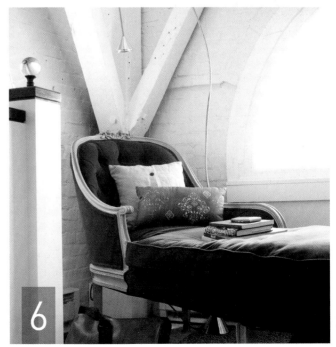

6

CHAPTER FIVE

sleep

beds & frames

a lthough what makes a bed comfortable is a matter of personal preference, what makes a bed fit comfortably in a room is not as subjective. If you try to squeeze a king-size mattress, which measures 76x80 inches, into a 9x10-foot bedroom, you might be able to fit a dresser in, too—but don't plan on opening the drawers. At 54x75 inches, a full-size bed will fit the space better, accommodate two people, and give you room for a dresser, nightstand, and maybe a chair.

Fortunately, you can have a wonderful headboard no matter the mattress size. Headboards take up little or no floor space and add style and personality to the room. Depending on the type you choose, a headboard can also contribute a vertical element that helps enlarge the sense of space.

◄ A headboard with posts stretches a small bedroom by playing up the vertical dimension. A chest used as a nightstand compensates for limited closet space and complements the handsome headboard.

↑ With a sleigh bed, the bedding tucks under the mattress to show off the beautiful wood frame. This creates a tailored, clean-lined look that minimizes visual clutter in a small room.

◄ In this bedroom the fabrics dominate, so the low headboard simply supports the pillows at an angle to play up their important role as color accents.

↑ **A four-poster bed** can make a small room feel more generous thanks to the "verticals are your friend" trick. The slender posts lead the eye upward, suggesting greater volume. Sheer fabric panels add a softening effect without interrupting sight lines that open up the space.

← **Capture attention with the headboard,** and the room's dimensions become secondary. This extra-tall upholstered headboard balances the visual weight of the bed and introduces the illusion of depth, while contributing an eye-catching pattern to the room.

→ **Spaces with low or angled ceilings work well for beds,** as you don't normally need room to stand up. Here, a low-to-the floor bed tucks neatly into an alcove and leaves room for a nightstand.

storage

L ying down to sleep in itself doesn't put a lot of storage demands on your small space, but you need a spot for certain bedside essentials, such as books, magazines, glasses, and an alarm clock. And when you drift off at night and wake up in the morning, it's comforting to be surrounded by favorite objects. A simple nightstand doesn't take up much space, nor does a headboard with built-in storage or a shelf or two on the wall. But the objects you place there help personalize what is already very personal space.

A smart strategy is to decorate your bedroom with furniture pieces that have storage capacity, such as an armoire. Armoires are available in a range of styles and sizes, and they feature drawers for stowing sweaters and blankets, plus clothing rods for hanging shirts, jackets, and trousers. Or place an upholstered ottoman with concealed storage at the foot of your bed. Unlike expensive built-ins or closet systems, bedroom furniture is portable and can move with you, which is ideal for renters.

◄ **A contemporary, molded-plywood bench** serves as a nightstand in a small apartment bedroom. The open design doesn't block heat from the radiator.

► **This bedroom never sleeps.** By day, it's a home office. The built-ins conserve square footage and do double duty, holding both work supplies and bedside items.

▼ **A wall-mount nightstand** frees up floor space, making the room feel more expansive because the eye can travel past the furniture to the edge of the room.

HOW TO:
PICK A NIGHTSTAND

Nightstands are most convenient when they're just a few inches above mattress height—typically 27–33 inches tall.

Consider how you'll use a nightstand and what you want to store or display. Items such as tissues, eyeglasses, and books may be easier to reach on shelves. But you might want to keep some things in a drawer.

No room for a nightstand? Hang a shallow shelf above the bed—one just deep enough for a lamp or an alarm clock.

wall treatments

blank white walls may make a space feel larger, but they also make it boring. Add artwork—either a single piece or a montage of collected items—and white becomes a canvas for your self-expression.
Painted beaded board or paneling can add texture and depth to walls and stamp your room with cottage or Craftsman style. In living rooms and dining rooms, the wainscot usually tops out at chair height, but in a bedroom try carrying the treatment three-quarters of the way up the wall (to frame the headboard) and install a plate rail. Lining the plate rail with artwork takes visual interest up the wall, increasing the room's perceived height.

If you like lots of pattern, consider wallpaper. Height-enhancing vertical stripes, small-scale patterns, or low-contrast designs can add interest and depth without overpowering the room. Don't be afraid of medium- to large-scale patterns—balanced with swaths of solid color, a large design can turn a boring little box into a fabulous retreat.

STRETCH SPACE WITH MOLDINGS

Moldings are one of the easiest ways to add style and character to a room. In a small bedroom, vertical molding on the walls creates the illusion of greater height, and the addition of crown molding calls attention to the ceiling, which also increases the apparent volume. Home centers offer a variety of premilled molding pieces that are easy to install. Paint or stain them to suit your bedroom's decor.

◄ **If you can't change white walls,** turn them into a canvas for art. Here, found works and family creations add color and depth, filling in for a headboard and hiding an electrical panel that couldn't be moved.

▼ **Horizontal paneling expands this bedroom** by wrapping around the walls and stretching their perceived length. Bands of white molding form a charming cottage contrast with the blue.

A balmy wall color creates a sense of calm and suggests skylike spaciousness.

REMOVABLE WALL TREATMENTS

If you can't paint or paper your bedroom walls, there are options for enhancing the small space. Removable wallpapers and decals add color and pattern and can be easily taken down. You can also cover entire walls with decorated sheets of canvas or muslin fabric. Many DIYers use liquid fabric starch to hang fabric on walls. The starch sticks without damaging the wall or the fabric.

A headboard is part of this room's wall treatment, pulling the eye upward and providing an expanse of calm amid the lively fabric wall covering. An extra-tall window treatment enhances the sense of height.

Offset the horizontal weight of the bed by creating vertical vitality on the wall behind. Suede-covered panels, an upholstered headboard, tall lamps, and a sunburst mirror all raise the level of interest.

bedding & pillows

I f the mattress and frame are the bones of your bed, then the bedding and pillows are the skin. In fact, they're what your skin touches, so it's important that these elements be super comfortable. But bedding also sets the style of a bedroom. And in a small sleeping space, where the bed tends to really dominate, linens and pillows carry outsize visual impact. They add layers to the decor, which makes the room more interesting.

Fortunately, bedding is one of the easiest—and most affordable— decorating elements to personalize. There are material and style choices to suit every budget and taste, whether you prefer crisp, classic white linens or bedding full of bright colors and bold patterns.

Don't overlook the power of pillows, either. They're not just a place to rest your head. Whether you use a couple or pile several on the bed, they offer a low-risk way to introduce room-changing color, pattern, and texture.

↑ **Choose bedding in solid colors** when other elements dazzle with their patterns. Here, the chandelier, curtains, and headboard energize the small room, while the brown and pink on the bed keep it grounded.

← **If you like crisp white sheets,** give the bed more personality by piling on pillows rich in color and texture. The tans and browns add depth to the sleeping space and complement furnishings and accessories.

➡ **Spreads and pillows are style-setters** in sleeping quarters, as in this floral-theme room. The flowery decor connects the bedroom to the outdoors, which seems to extend the boundaries of the space.

Let bedding cue the colors of accessories to create a unifying, calming look.

Bedspread: Falls to the floor on the sides and end. Light colors and minimal patterns are the most space-enhancing.

Comforter: Filled with down or a synthetic material, this thick but lightweight option covers only the mattress, so it's best teamed with a skirt that hides the box springs and underbed area.

Coverlet: Similar to a comforter but usually lighter weight.

Duvet: Basically a comforter encased in a removable cover—like a giant pillowcase—that protects it and keeps it clean.

Quilt: A stitched coverlet with two layers and padding. A quilt can also be used as a blanket or folded at the foot of the bed.

Striving to blend color and calm is a smart decorating approach in a small bedroom, where you want the look to be restful but not boring. The bedding here is mostly in solid colors, though two pillows pick up the energy of the curtains and wall art.

Modern and traditional styles meet in this happy combination of a botanical-print comforter and classic toile headboard and bed skirt. Height-stretching paneling picks up the soft color of the toile, giving it just a little more weight than the citrusy green bedding.

lighting

ighting is a tricky subject in a bedroom. If you're trying to sleep, too much light is a distraction. But if you're trying to wake up—or get dressed—lighting helps. And if you like to read before bed or use your sleeping quarters as living space (such as an office) by day, you want a certain amount of task and general room lighting in stylish forms.

A small home presents even more of a bedroom lighting challenge. Without adequate natural light, a small bedroom feels dark and cramped. But large windows complicate bed and furniture placement. Fortunately, it doesn't take a lot of light—natural or artificial—to illuminate a small space. And your options—ceiling fixtures, table lamps, and wall sconces—don't have to take up much space. Yet the fixtures themselves can add to the decorating style of your bedroom, even as they shine light on other elements.

◄ Certain lamps flatter small spaces.
This one echoes the slender shape of the
tapered bedpost, helping direct the eye
upward. The white shade complements the
wallpaper pattern and bed linens.

➤ Small bedrooms love natural light.
A corner window and a light wall color
combine to soften this room's boundaries. A
chandelier draws attention to the ceiling, and
a lamp eases bedtime reading.

DESIGN BASICS:
LIGHT HEIGHT

Position a bedside reading lamp
so the bottom of the shade
is about 20 inches above the
mattress. At that height the light
should clearly illuminate the
page when you're reading in bed
but not cast glare in your eyes.

↑ **Swag lamps are smart and stylish** in a small bedroom. They don't take up any floor space or require a tabletop, yet they can light up fairly large areas and their shades offer an opportunity to add color and personality.

← **Daylight and fixtures work together** to make this small bedroom spacious and special. The nearly floor-to-ceiling window extends the space into the outdoors, while the modern chandelier provides a focal point.

Bedroom lamps don't have to be large to make a big impact. The pair flanking this bed fit on small nightstands yet brighten the small space even when they're turned off.

Wall sconces are a good choice for small bedrooms, saving floor and tabletop space as they direct attention to the upper portions of the walls.

colors & patterns

though your actual sleep mileage may vary, it is true that you spend about one-third of your life in bed, so the surrounding space should be one you feel comfortable in and enjoy looking at, especially first thing in the morning and last thing at night. Color and pattern are your allies, whether you need a jump start in the morning or help unwinding at night.

For the color scheme, start with an existing rug, wallpaper, or paint color. Or find a favorite fabric or piece of art to anchor your overall color scheme. Ideally, each color in the original object should be repeated at least once in the room. But don't feel compelled to match the colors perfectly.

The same favorite element can cue patterns, too. Aim for a mix of small, medium, and large-scale patterns. And make sure all of your patterns have at least one color that is similar, even if it is a background or neutral. In a room with multiple patterns, make sure there's a place for the eye to rest, ideally a white or neutral color that separates and highlights the patterns.

DESIGN BASICS:
TEXTURE MATTERS

Texture is decorating you can feel, and it's key in a bedroom, a place where your skin meets surfaces as you dress, groom, go barefoot, and lie down. In a small bedroom, texture adds depth and detail without demanding extra space. Every surface or material imparts a texture.

By varying the types— smooth, coarse, fibrous, metallic—you create the sense that there's more than meets the eye. And that's the heart of small-space decorating.

↑ **By repeating a favorite pattern,** you connect different elements in the room and add a layer of design depth. The intersecting lines of the star light fixture echo in one of the pillows and the cabinet doors.

← **If you think white is boring,** think again. This white-on-white bedroom layers shades of ivory, snow, and cream to create a serene space that would feel expansive even if it didn't have access to a deck.

➡ **Tap the power of patterns and colors** to draw attention where you want it. In this bedroom, the window behind the bed opens up the space on that wall. The eye-catching curtains and pillows frame the window.

CASE STUDY #5

budget chic

You can decorate a tight space on a tight budget without sacrificing style. Relying on favorite colors, found objects, and economical solutions, the occupant of this 900-square-foot apartment created a look that's personable, functional, and affordable. See how to put your best foot forward on a shoestring budget.

1

2

1 **Stained-glass panels on the bedroom windows** had been added by a previous tenant to hide views of the neighbor's home. Moving the bed under the window panels made them an extension of the headboard.

2 **Using white as a base color for furnishings** keeps the look light and creates a flexible decorating canvas—it's easy to switch out pillows, throws, and art. Slender table and chair legs foster an open feel.

3 **Copper sheeting is a stylish disguise** for an unsightly fireplace surround in the dining room. The copper complements the wood tones of the table and buffet, which are sized to serve without crowding the space.

4 **When creating a montage wall of art,** pay attention to the spaces between the items—varying them slightly will create a more dynamic composition. To keep the overall effect orderly, anchor the bottom row to an architectural element (like the pass-through frame) or a piece of furniture. This high-profile space between the living room and kitchen begged for personalizing, and the renter did it with favorite prints and colors. Inside the kitchen, laminated art paper proved a quick and easy way to cover ugly tile.

5 **To create a space within a small space,** use an area rug to define a furniture grouping. This office tucks into a spot by the bay window, where there's natural light to work in and a view for inspiration.

CHAPTER SIX

work

desks & chairs

desk space and some type of chair are the only things you really need to work at home, but in a small dwelling, finding room for even those minimal elements can be a challenge. It helps if you're creative in finding a location and willing to let your office work part-time. That way, it can share square footage and be multifunctional.

The kitchen, a bedroom, a hallway, or even a closet are all potential spots for office space. A corner of a living or dining room often works well. Choose the smallest desktop you can comfortably use. This could be a freestanding furniture piece you buy or part of an existing built-in or countertop. Even a shelving unit can be turned into a desk.

For the chair, you're free to go beyond traditional office furniture. Upholstered pieces avoid an institutional look, and when desk space is near a living or dining area, you may be able to borrow a chair from there. If you prefer a dedicated desk chair, make sure it complements the room's decor.

A dressing table or vanity can double as a desk. A well-lit corner of the bedroom provides a favorable setting for both functions. And the place where you sleep is often where you think of things you should write down.

Glass or acrylic desks are good choices for small spaces, as the transparent surfaces render a home office virtually invisible. This one fits neatly into wall space between two doorways. The chair fits the modern vibe.

Using an upholstered chair at the desk creates a furnished look that doesn't announce "office space." The white desk/table blends into the decor, and the open space below it adds breathing room.

When a desk offers limited storage, a freestanding shelf unit provides a boost.

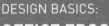

DESIGN BASICS:
OFFICE ERGONOMICS

Whatever your office setup, the height of the chair should let your feet rest comfortably on the floor, with your knees about level with your hips. Any computer screen should be 18–30 inches from your eyes—about an arm's length away. The top of the screen should be at eye level or below so that you look down slightly at your work. Try to avoid glare from windows or overhead lighting.

↑ **A foldable desk offers flexibility** in allocating work space and living space. This desk can be easily moved or removed without leaving a decorating void. The shelves behind incorporate office items into accessories.

➡ **A built-in office saves space** by tucking the desk and chair into a wall niche. The design is especially popular in kitchens, where cabinetry and countertop materials repeat in the desk storage and work surface.

To maximize corner office space, do away with the desk entirely and opt for a shelf that's cantilevered or supported by brackets. The design leaves open space below for storage and files.

Any recess within a living area offers potential space for a workstation. This one fits into a niche next to a fireplace, where the typical bookcase was tweaked to accommodate a computer and chair.

storage

your work-at-home spot needs some kind of storage, whether it's just a little space for a few office supplies or extensive room for books, files, and equipment. In a small home, it's important to store only what you really need, to organize it well, to keep it where you can see it, and to focus on built-ins and vertical space.

To keep a small desk clutter-free, try stacking simple trays on top for items you want in sight and in mind, such as bills and outgoing mail. Use a file box to hold items you need to access regularly, such as receipts and contact information.

When storage needs are greater, one approach is to discreetly extend the office into the surrounding room or an adjacent space. For example, a kitchen desk could claim a cabinet or drawer in the cooking area for storage, and an office in the living room might annex part of a bookcase.

Wheels make a desk chair easy to move somewhere else for quick extra seating.

◄ Bookcases can provide double-duty storage near desk space. In this living room, the shelves hold not only general books, collectibles, and accessories, but also specific volumes and files for office business.

↑ A combination of wall-hung shelves, drawers, and cubbies turns a corner into an efficient office. Even the desk is a model of do-it-yourself simplicity.

Drawers can be space-efficient storage solutions in an office area, but not if you use them as catchalls. Streamline drawers periodically by emptying the contents and deciding what to keep, toss, and move. Then use a drawer organizer with movable dividers to neatly arrange the "keepers." Refill—but don't overfill—each drawer, placing often-used items up front and lesser-used items toward the back.

When an office occupies a corner of the kitchen, continuing the countertop material and cabinetry style creates a unified look. And the space can be converted to an extra kitchen prep station or serving area.

Going vertical is a reliable small-space storage approach. Here, normally bare upper walls hold tiers of shelves above a compact office. Tree-pattern wallpaper provides subtle background and interest.

The multi-use mantra of small-space living means grouping an office with related functions. That could be in a laundry or utility area, alongside other items that keep the home clean, neat, and organized.

personal touches

I n a twist on the old adage, all work and no play makes for a dull home office. It is a *home* office, after all, so the decor should reflect at least as much homeyness as office-ness, if not more so. That's where personal touches become important. In a small home, there are fewer spaces available to make a decorating impact, and each one carries a greater weight than it would in a larger dwelling. So don't take a pass by letting your office space be generic. Make it a stylish part of the home and a reflection of your tastes and personality.

Personalizing office space means considering everything from the color of the wall and the shape of the desk and chair to what you put on the shelves and the floor. What kind of work environment suits you? You may like lots of colors and patterns for stimulation, or you may prefer a quieter visual field. Do you want to work in private or in a more public part of the home? There are many ways to make a small office space truly yours.

Fun colors and expressive geometry give this small office space big personality. Curtains hide the niche when desired, but they draw back to let in natural light. A mirror expands the space visually.

Favorite artwork and colorful accessories personalize this desk area. Though the look is formal, the little bursts of color avoid a staid feel. And the mirror keeps the corner spot from seeming confining.

This desk space occupies only a few feet, but it's packed with personal touches. Shelves trimmed with cork appear to float on the wall, and the stool can be a grab-and-go extra seat elsewhere.

Business need not be boring. A zebra-pattern rug and polka dot bench are cheeky choices that play off the high-contrast color palette.

DESIGN BASICS:
OPTIMIZING AN OFFICE

To create a home office you'll be comfortable and productive in, be sure to provide light, color, and inspiration.

For light, try to incorporate at least two artificial sources. Typically, that means a desk lamp in addition to an overhead fixture. Any natural light you can draw in is a bonus.

For color, think about which hues will allow you to be most productive and creative. Bright colors may stimulate and invigorate, but they could wear out your eyes after a while. Softer shades usually make it easier to focus.

For inspiration, include a few items that will motivate you and add a positive vibe, such as family photos, art, mementos, quotes, and awards.

CASE STUDY #6
family function

Bucking the bigger-is-better approach to new homes, this suburban dwelling gives a young family the spaces they need while maintaining modest dimensions. Built-ins, beaded board, and a sense of separate rooms channel old-house charm and character in a flexible floor plan that makes the most of the square footage.

1

1 **Small, easily moved tables** let the living room double as a children's play zone. When the kids are indoors for the winter, the homeowners like to store puzzles and board games under the sofa for quick access.

2 **The small entry is also a mini mudroom,** thanks to a built-in coatrack with beaded-board detailing that reflects the home's architectural character. A swath of floor below is a drop zone for shoes and bags.

3 **The compact dining room** provides a dedicated space for family meals. Chairs with slender frames minimize visual weight, while tall windows with simple treatments enhance spaciousness.

4 **By day, this corner of the master bedroom** works as a cozy family reading spot. Built-ins hold books, magazines, and accessories. The kids can use the ottoman as another place to sit.

5 **A multipurpose island** boosts counter space in what's essentially a one-wall kitchen. Besides holding the sink, the island top is great for serving buffet-style meals and hosting pizza-making nights.

6 **Space-saving banquette seating** makes it possible to squeeze a breakfast nook into the kitchen. A big window extends the visual boundaries of the space, and the nook augments kitchen prep areas and provides additional guest seating at parties.

CHAPTER SEVEN

multitask

loft living

downtown dwellings are the epitome of loft living—think digs carved out of the upper floors of an old warehouse or office building. But you can experience loft-style living in practically any kind of small home. It could be space above a garage, up in an attic, down in the basement, or in an apartment, condo, or townhome.

What loft spaces have in common are minimal interior walls, high or angled ceilings, and exposed structural elements such as beams, columns, ductwork, and conduits. Though these qualities create openness and character in a small space, they also present a decorating challenge. The furnishings and accessories you choose must be able to support a variety of activities yet maintain a cohesive look when seen all at once.

The most appealing lofts embrace their eccentricities and make them part of the decorating scheme. By subdividing the open space and incorporating versatile yet vibrant furnishings, you can multitask in style.

LOFT STORAGE

Loft-style spaces have few interior walls, making storage difficult to find. But lofts usually have long stretches of exterior wall space and odd-shape nooks that carry storage potential. Long, tall bookcases work well on the perimeter, as do cabinets, shelves, and drawers that tuck under a sloping ceiling. Toward the middle of the room, stick to low-profile pieces that combine furniture and storage functions, such as a trunk-turned-coffee-table.

Sleeping, working, and relaxing are all supported by this loft-style above-garage apartment. A pole-mounted TV swivels to let the screen face different areas of the space. The back side holds books and DVDs.

Lofts don't demand modern style. Traditional kitchen cabinetry and living room furniture balance the industrial interiors with elegance, while colors and finishes complement the exposed ductwork. The placement of a rug and sofa separates the living area from the kitchen.

A two-color paint scheme accents the ceiling height.

Paneling a structurally necessary column turns it into a stylish room divider for a loft. Space under the peaked ceiling works well for a desk area with storage.

flexible furniture

furniture pieces that do more than one thing are an absolute boon when you're decorating a small space. Some multitasking pieces, such as the sleeper sofa, have been around for decades, but other pieces—the ottoman that doubles as a storage bin, the coffee table that pops up to make a dining table—reflect manufacturers' response to consumer needs.

Even without the aid of ready-made multipurpose furniture, you can adapt your own pieces through creative repurposing. Need a bedside table? Put a side chair to work. When you need the chair for extra seating in the living room, it's easy enough to move. Modular storage cubes stack to form room dividers. A skinny table does butler duty in an entry, a bath, a hallway, or a dining room, and stacked garden benches become instant bookshelves.

Portability and adjustability are priorities for small-space furnishings, but looks matter, too. When a furniture piece wears a color, pattern, or finish that works in a variety of settings, that makes it versatile, too.

This mod-look space is made for multitasking. The futons work as sofas or beds, the square ottomans serve as tables or seats, and the round table can host any activity.

Furnishings that switch roles and places earn their spots in a small space. Here, a trunk is an entertainment stand, an ottoman is a coffee table, and a kitchen cart is a wheeled bookcase.

This leather sofa table is stylish and versatile, offering lamp and display space on top as well as storage in the drawers and below. Pull up one or both of the stools, and it can be a temporary desk or dining spot.

FLEX FAVORITES

These furniture pieces are especially valuable in a small home, where they can save space by doing double duty.

Armchair: When you have one that's modest in size yet big enough to be comfortable, it can work in a conversation group, move to an office area, or sit at the head of a dining table.

Ottoman: The MVP of multitasking, the ottoman props up feet, holds books and dishes, and provides extra seating. Keep it lightweight, and you can easily slide it where it's needed.

Round table: Is it a dining table? A coffee table? A side table? An end table? Yes. The shape frees up space and eases traffic flow.

Anything on wheels: A rolling piece puts things where you need them when you need them. It could be a kitchen or bath storage cart with casters or a wheeled coffee table that moves out to open up the living room.

room dividers

t's a challenge to make your small home look large and still get all the function you need out of it. One of the biggest issues is how—and how much—you should divide up the space. Clearly, too many interior walls make a small home seem even smaller, but it's also true that a lack of structural and visual boundaries can create problems with noise, privacy, storage, and traffic flow.

Fortunately, there are ways to subdivide a small space without creating the proverbial rabbit warren. Furniture is your best ally. Long or tall pieces such as sofas, bookcases, and armoires can fill in for walls, creating smaller "rooms" within a single open space. You can delineate an entry foyer in a home that lacks one, or partially enclose a sleeping area in an apartment without a separate bedroom.

Decorating choices can define spaces, too. A change in wall color or the placement of a rug can mark the transition from one area to another.

A sofa is a natural room divider, as its length and shape frame seating groups and direct traffic around either end. This room features another good small-space divider: a partition with a window opening.

DESIGN BASICS:
FOLDING DIVIDERS

One of the simplest and most stylish ways to separate spaces in a small home is with folding screens and dividers. These freestanding, multi-panel units go anywhere you want privacy or separation, and it's easy to move and remove them as desired. Though highly functional, folding dividers are also highly decorative, giving you the opportunity to add color, pattern, and texture. Wood and fabric are the most common materials, but glass and metal are striking, too.

Bookcases make good walls in a small home, dividing rooms and providing storage while maintaining openness. Here, a hutchlike partition extends the divider to the ceiling but keeps the look light.

When a wall doesn't completely separate one room from another, the decor can reinforce boundaries. In this home, a rugged wall frames the sitting area, but it's the rug that anchors the furniture grouping.

Partial walls divide spaces without confining them.

color schemes

you can use color as a unifying force when a single space is used for a variety of different activities. When different areas within a room serve different functions, the colors you choose can set off each area and give it a little different personality. At the same time, keeping some colors the same from area to area promotes unity.

Often, a consistent wall color is the simplest and most effective unifying thread in a small home. That doesn't mean all your walls have to be the same color, but when physical distance between spaces is minimal, subtle and gradual color changes usually work best to maintain openness. If you do opt for multiple wall colors, keep moldings and trim the same color.

You can also achieve color unity by limiting the palette to a few colors and using them in different amounts and intensities in different areas. When you keep walls uniformly calm, let furniture, fabrics, and accessories supply the color power.

Color unites this multitasking space. Although it's separated into living and dining areas, consistent wall color and similar wood tones ease the transition. The color shift from the rug to hardwood flooring is gentle.

Subtle wall-color differences work best in a small home. Here, white upper walls with a golden wainscoting give way to a creamier neutral in the room through the doorway, differentiating the spaces while uniting them.

A change in wall color sets off the dining portion of this combined space from the living area. The green wall draws on the scenery outdoors, helping expand the space. Repeating wood tones create cohesion.

DESIGN BASICS:
SMALL-SPACE COLOR

Don't be afraid to use color in a small space, but do handle it with care. Here are some tips.

White's not always right: For walls, try a medium-range color like a warm green or yellow instead. Leave upper walls white and paint bright, light colors on the wainscoting.

Rugs rule: Rugs are a great way to add color in a small space. Choose simple patterns that pick up the wall hue. Stripes will elongate the room.

Pillows are potent portables: Large, colorful pillows energize small living and family rooms. They supply extra casual seating, too.

Windows need to breathe: Dark, heavy draperies or layers of window treatments break up walls and block light, shrinking a small room. Go with light-color shades or simple sheer curtains.

Dark-wood flooring is a drag: A light stain reflects better than a dark stain, so it makes the room seem bigger. If you have dark floors, try covering them with light or neutral rugs. Or go with a white-on-white scheme and let the floor be a dramatic anchor.

studio drama

Small spaces are the norm in New York City, where urban dwellers excel at squeezing style and function from precious square footage. In this studio apartment, a designer's eye for proportion, flair for drama, and desire for a double-duty space produced a home of simple colors and elaborate details.

1

1 Multi-use is mandatory in a small home, and this apartment shows how to do it artfully. When both faux-bamboo chairs are at the table, this spot is a dining area for two with a view of the city. But pull one chair to the table at the left and you have a corner office. Push the two tables together to serve buffet-style.

2 A simple black-and-white color scheme punctuated by gold and brown accents creates drama and sophistication. Above the desk space, oversize frames and wide mats enhance the artistic quality of the varied images on display.

3 **A small sofa tucks into a corner of the main living area,** and its white upholstery blends into the walls for a space-enhancing look. The sofa is comfortably big enough without dominating the room, while small, easily movable tables allow for versatility when entertaining. Oversize pillows can be changed seasonally to bring in the desired color and patterns. The wooden wall hanging is an antique Chinese window incorporating the symbol of longevity. Wall sconces save space by eliminating the need for end tables and lamps.

4 **Don't be afraid to use a dark wall color in a small home.** The charcoal in the bedroom provides a sleep-friendly backdrop in an otherwise bright apartment. The dark color also lets gold frames and accessories glitter while calling out the crispness of the bedding. The divider allows a TV to be viewed from different angles.

5 **A pedestal sink saves space in the bath** while conveying a sophisticated look. The frameless design of the mirrored medicine cabinet and the mirrored backing for the shelves present an illusion of greater depth. A fabric shower curtain softens the look.

CHAPTER EIGHT

enter

welcoming

the entry of your small home is more than just a way to get in and out. If you think of your front door as a guard, then the space just inside is a greeter, welcoming guests when they arrive and bidding them farewell when they depart. Pretend you're a guest walking into your home for the first time. How does the decor near the door greet you? Is it a warm embrace, an effusive handshake, a quiet nod and smile, or an indifferent stare? Whatever the feeling, it sets the tone for the entire home.

Even if your entry is small or virtually nonexistent, you can still use it to make a style statement. The message just has to be concise. Try creating a small vignette of furnishings to give a sneak peek into the mix of styles that lies beyond. Put your favorite antiques and collectibles on display. Hang a striking light fixture, or place a favorite lamp on a table for a warm glow. Plants or fresh flowers are a welcoming touch, too. Remember, your home gets only one chance to make a first impression.

◄— A shelf to hold a mirror and flowers takes up little room yet makes an entry pretty and practical. There's room on the shelf for incoming and outgoing items. A coat tree is practical and eats little space.

—► A charming entry is a preview for your home's coming attractions. Here, the decor promises a casual, colorful cottage look. The narrow table lengthens the space.

Objects near the entry should hint at your home's style.

↑ Mirrors are good choices for entries because their reflections fool the eye into seeing more space than what's actually there. In this home, they're also part of a vignette that greets guests with a bold style message.

◄— Natural light boosts spaciousness in an entry area. If your front door is blessed with sidelights or window panels, leave the openings bare for a clean, bright look. A bench by the door makes it easy to take off or put on shoes before entering or exiting.

storage

ocation, location, location. To paraphrase an old real-estate adage, those are the three most important factors to consider when planning storage—i.e., you keep things where you need them. This point-of-use approach is especially practical in an entry area. Next to the door is the best place to store the things you need when you go out into the world.

Even the smallest entry can serve as a pickup/drop-off station. A wall-mount console table fits nicely in a narrow space, providing a spot for mail and keys on arrival, and a small bench adjacent to it is appreciated when putting on or taking off shoes and boots.

If you like to hide family gear handsomely, place an armoire by the door. For a more open look, mount a set of cubbies on the wall and use them to store hats, gloves, scarves, balls, and bags. Don't have that much space to spare? Try a coat tree or umbrella stand to cash in on vertical space. Even a few wall-mount hooks can keep coats and jackets where you need them.

MAKE A MINI MUDROOM

Create mudroom-style storage on a few feet of wall space by your entry. Install a 1x6 board about 5 feet above the floor and attach a row of metal coat hooks. Or, instead of coat hooks, attach a metal storage rod and use S hooks to hang backpacks, keys, shopping bags, and storage baskets. If you have the space, add a wall shelf above the rod and use baskets to hold gloves, scarves, and hats.

This colorful stand catches eyes and gear. Its height makes smart use of vertical space, while its slim back hugs the wall to avoid crowding the entry. The cutouts and vibrant shade set a fun tone.

When entry storage blends into the look of the room, it boosts function and style in the same small space. These rugged shelves are perfect for the rustic decor.

Even a few feet of space by the door can be a storage bonanza when you use the entire wall and customize the space to what you need to store. These bins on wheels wear a colorful mix of patterns, to boot.

open & cozy

You can have it both ways in a small home, enjoying the coziness of compact rooms with all the light and openness of a larger dwelling. That's what a couple found when they moved into this Minnesota home. Its lake-cottage-look spaces promote family togetherness while giving everyone room to breathe.

1

2

1 **Natural light and muted colors** make the modest-size living room a peaceful escape. The coffee table's open frame builds in breathing space, and the white armchair can go where needed. Its zebra-print fabric injects a little wildness into the rustic look.

2 **Built-ins save space in a small home** and provide versatile storage. These bookcases hold more than just books, and their low height keeps them from looming over the room and blocking out the light. The wood tones complement the floor and furniture.

3 **Soft colors and a bank of windows** foster spaciousness in the fairly small master bedroom. The table by the windows offers all-purpose storage and display space. It can even serve as a makeshift desk.

4 **A built-in microwave saves counter space** in the kitchen, where painting base cabinets white lightened the once oak-heavy look. A doorless cupboard adds to the open feeling, as does the subway-tile backsplash.

5 **The banquette is another space-saver,** its bench seating several people in a compact area. Upholstered chairs can move into the living room when there's a crowd or pull up to the trestle table for casual meals or games.

6 **A glass-door hutch and wicker chairs** accentuate airiness in the dining room. The height of the hutch and the wainscot molding help the room stand tall, while the painted-twig chandelier conveys personality.

CHAPTER NINE

play

theme rooms

having children in your home, whether all the time or just for occasional visits, gives you an excuse to indulge in some fun decorating. Kids' bedrooms and play areas call for lively, colorful looks that stimulate the imagination and make the spaces fun and comforting to be in. And while these spaces may be small, their dimensions needn't limit how creative you can be in furnishing them.

One approach is to develop a theme for the room. Children have their passions—favorite books, TV shows, movies, hobbies—and they like it when their rooms reflect those. Though some interests are intense but short-lived, others may be the start of a lifelong pursuit. And some classic themes and decor will always hold appeal for kids. Think outer space, dollhouses, fire trucks, animals, race cars, flowers, cowboys, and sports.

Fortunately, it doesn't take a lot of elements to establish a theme in a small space. And your little ones will appreciate a little personalization.

In a small home, kids might share a room. In that case, let each child choose one of the main colors in the overall scheme. Use accessories to blend the favorites. Separate beds can be dressed alike while still recognizing each child's personality. For example, try the same pattern on each bed but in different colors. Or use reversible comforters with different sides facing up. Color coding can reduce arguments by keeping belongings separate.

Objects hung from the ceiling are fun and make good use of vertical space. Here, the solar system is colorful and educational, just like the map over the window and the globe by the bed.

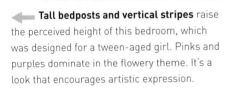

Tall bedposts and vertical stripes raise the perceived height of this bedroom, which was designed for a tween-aged girl. Pinks and purples dominate in the flowery theme. It's a look that encourages artistic expression.

A light hand with a red, white, and blue color scheme allows this room to shift focus with a few changes in accessories. A farm-motif rug, bed quilt, and star-emblazoned pillows say "country." Replace them with sailboats and lighthouses, and the theme becomes nautical.

made-to-grow decor

t's been said that children's rooms are gardens for their imaginations and dreams. The best ones are those made to grow with their occupants. So think twice before adding an intricate mural that kids will soon decide is too juvenile, or buying an elaborate bed canopy that will get torn apart when used as a jungle gym. Try to make the space a simple yet whimsical canvas for constantly changing tastes and interests.

In a small home, it make sense to keep the basic elements and main furniture pieces of kids' rooms simple and classic. That way they can be reused in style updates over the years. Take advantage of accessories and other easily changed features to reflect changing themes.

Even if the children are small now, try to envision them in their grade-school years and beyond, busy with schoolwork, friends, and activities. Choose decor that can be tweaked as they move through tween and teen years. And let them help choose the looks they like—and you can live with.

Upholstered headboards lend sophisticated color and softness to a child's bedroom.

◄ **This close-to-the floor bed** is at a good height for younger kids, yet it's big enough for older ones, too. And its low profile works well in a room with a sloping ceiling. White walls let bedding and accessories supply the color.

► **Designed for younger girls,** this shared small bedroom works for teens, too. The upholstered headboards, bed skirts, and Roman shade are all sophisticated, grown-up touches, yet saturated with color.

DESIGN BASICS:
BEDS FOR KIDS

As soon as children outgrow their cribs, their beds become the focal points of their rooms, setting the style tone. Resist the temptation to get too cute with the choice. A car-shape bed is fun for a little kid, but not so much for a middle-schooler— or an adult guest using the room for the night. Well-made, full-size beds and furniture will serve children for years. And in a small home, those pieces make the space more versatile when the nest is empty.

► **The simpler you keep the basic look,** the easier it is for the room to grow with the child. In this boy's room, a basic yet sturdy bed and a brown-based color scheme provide a setting suitable for a younger or older child.

storage

On the metal buckets (labels): Race Cars · Little Men · Big Men

On the drawers (labels): Army Men & Weapons · Army Trucks · Stuffed · Stuffed Animals

Music

Weapons

f or adults, kids' rooms often embody all the hopes and dreams they have for the children in their lives. They spend much time, energy, and money trying to create perfect incubators for the children's vast potential. Of course, reality eventually hits, and the rooms become repositories for lots of stuff—scattered toys with tiny parts, a wardrobe of clothes that may or may not fit anymore, and a certain amount of unidentifiable debris under the bed. Storing it all neatly is a challenge, especially if the room is small.

The goal with kids' room storage is to make toys, clothes, and supplies easily accessible so that the kids don't have to yell for help finding things, and they might even put them away—and in the right place.

Toy boxes and big baskets can contain large odds and ends, but small things tend to disappear to the bottom. Consider desk and office organizers, as well as some storage designed especially for kids. For clothes, dressers and armoires work fine, but drawers are easier to keep neat than shelves.

⬅ Good perimeter storage saves space in a small bedroom. These colorful buckets work well for small items. The labels help kids stay organized and reinforce their spelling and reading skills.

⬆ Capitalize on low ceilings in attics and upper-level bedrooms. The wall nooks and niches underneath are great for storage, leaving the full-height center of the room open for play.

DESIGN BASICS:
CUT KIDS' CLUTTER

Only so many stuffed animals, toy trucks, beat-up books, and old clothes fit in a small room. Here's how to reduce that volume of clutter.

Daily: Set aside 10 minutes in the morning to tidy up.

Weekly: Establish housekeeping goals and put important chores on the calendar.

Monthly: Go through school papers and decide what to save in a memory box. Toss the rest.

Seasonally: Donate clothing kids have outgrown.

Twice a year: Go through toys, toss what's broken, and donate what's no longer needed.

Kitchen cabinets built into the wall take advantage of unused crawlspace in this upstairs bedroom. If built-ins aren't possible, consider anchoring cabinets to the wall and adding a laminate or wood countertop.

Kids have treasures to display, too, so include shelves for photos, trophies, souvenirs, and collectibles. Here, white shelves flank space-saving bunk beds and contrast nicely with orange walls.

Modular storage lets you customize shapes to the space. These big bedside wall cubbies fit neatly around the window, with one shelf doubling as a simple nightstand. Items are contained but easy to see.

In lieu of a window seat, these built-in cabinets put storage at a kid-friendly height. Removing the lower berth of a bunk bed opens plenty of storage space beneath the remaining mattress.

index

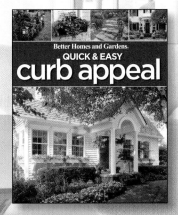

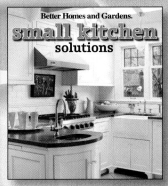
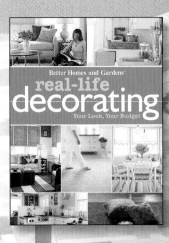

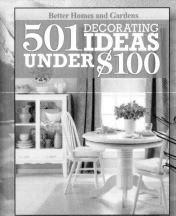